STEP-BY-STEP

macramé

A Complete Introduction to the Craft of Creative Knotting

By Mary Walker Phillips

Conceived and edited by
William and Shirley Sayles

GOLDEN PRESS ⬧ **NEW YORK**

WESTERN PUBLISHING COMPANY, INC.

Foreword

It can be said that we live in a world occupied with the exploration of construction techniques—a world not particularly romantic or introspective. Within the present decade weavers have been increasingly exploring the possibilities of constructing fabrics without the aid of a loom. Exhibitions of contemporary textiles include non-woven fabrics and forms in a variety of techniques. In addition, many of the fabrics used for clothing and furnishing are non-woven, and designers predict that their use will increase in the future. The fact that Mary Walker Phillips began her professional career as a weaver and fabric designer, and is now recognized as our foremost creative knitter, establishes her as a leading force in the current movement to explore non-woven constructions. Her interest in Macramé has been in part the result of her understanding and response to fibers and yarns and her adventure into research and delight in discovery.

Interest in knots has ranged from the intricacies of Leonardo da Vinci's interlacings, outlining complex Renaissance theories, to the fanciful fringes and embellishments of the Victorian era. Many cultures, ancient and contemporary, have used knotting as a means of fabric construction or decoration. This includes ritual masks of tribal Africa and fringes on Mexican shawls. Perhaps the most vital heritage, however, has been that of the sailor. Sailors, who have spent their lives with rope, twine, and cord and their interlacings and fastenings, have named countless numbers of knots. They have spent endless hours tying knots as part of their livelihood and as a means of pleasure. Few are aware of the fanciful and creative forms knotted by sailors in their spare time.

Mary Walker Phillips is fascinated by the relationship of the uncomplicated process of tying a knot to the clear and direct form of the knot itself. In the process of knotting she ties, re-ties, and constructs to produce an infinite variety of textures and shapes. Not always content with pure form, however, she adds the dimension of function and insists on a high standard of craftsmanship. This book was conceived and written to present clearly outlined projects in Macramé—projects which demonstrate the possibilities of the technique and the variety of functional and non-functional forms which can be created. The emphasis is on the response of the eye and the hand, and, ultimately, the individuality of the craftsman and the unique qualities of his work.

MILTON SONDAY
Assistant Curator of Textiles
Cooper-Hewitt Museum of Design,
Smithsonian Institution

Contents

INTRODUCTION	4
EQUIPMENT	10
YARNS	11
PROJECT PREVIEWS	12
PREPARING THE YARN	14
KNOTS	
Square Knot, Half Knot	16
Half Hitch, Overhand Knot,	18
Double Chain Knot	18
Double Half Hitch—Horizontal	20
Double Half Hitch—Vertical, Diagonal	21
Double Half Hitch—Angling Technique	22
Headings and Picots	24
FINISHING—FRINGE; SPLICING	25
TEXTURE	26
COLOR AND DESIGN	28
PROJECTS	
Hanging Planters	30
Tote Bag	32
PATIO HANGINGS	34
PROJECTS	
Placemat	36
Bracelets and Beads	38
Room Divider	40
Pillow Cover	42
TWO EXAMPLES FROM MITLA	44

PROJECTS	
Sash 1 (Jute Sash)	46
Sash 2 (Multicolor Sash)	48
Belts 1 and 2	50
Rugs	
Blue and Gold Rug	52
Red Rug	54
Cavandoli Stitch	56
Wall Hanging or Purse	58
WALL HANGINGS PORTFOLIO	
Spirit of '76	60
Amigo	61
Bill's Folly, Animal Fair	62
Peking	64
Empress	66
Summer Sun	67
Stately Mansion	68
Christmas Bells, project	70
Cascade	72
Nightbird	74
Gazebo	76
INDEX	78
BIBLIOGRAPHY AND BOOK SERVICES	79
SUPPLIERS	79
SCHOOLS AND WORKSHOPS	80

ACKNOWLEDGMENTS

Among those who have assisted in the preparation of this book, special thanks are due to:

Remo Cosentino, *Design and Production*
Louis Mervar, *Photography*
Paul Goodfriend Associates, *Diagrams*

Introduction

Sylvia's Book of Macramé Lace, published in England in the 1880's, states that "Goethe, somewhere or other, in exalting music above every other art, does so on the ground that it produces its marvellous effects with so little display of means and tools; and if this test be applied to our present work, it will rank very high . . . not even a thimble and needle, are wanted to produce the charming effects of our Macramé work."

Macramé can be practiced wherever you are, needing no more space than your lap. The knots themselves are also simple and can be easily followed from the diagrams given in this book.

KNOTS

Only two basic knots are involved—the Half Knot and the Half Hitch—but it is the endless variations on these two knots that generate all the excitement in Macramé. The wonder of this craft is that anything as simple as these two knots can produce such a variety of beautiful things, and such fun in making them. It is no surprise that both those who have become devoted to Macramé and those who are newly initiated find it difficult to leave their knotting boards.

Macramé has been defined as the interknotting of yarns. It is, however, much more than that in terms of the satisfaction that you will discover in the actual process of creating. The work is easier than it seems; a knowledge of knots is all that is necessary to make the most difficult-appearing knotting pattern.

This craft is now in the midst of an enthusiastic revival, and I would like to mention Virginia I. Harvey as one who has made a large contribution to this resurgence of interest. I had already explored this craft before seeing her book, *Macramé: The Art of Creative Knotting*, but, like lots of others, I have benefited greatly from it.

Many of us who had been busy in other crafts are now using this particular medium for several levels of expression—to create works of art, such as the wall hanging shown at left, and to make practical items for the home, such as the projects included in this book. Macramé is for all, for young and old, male and female—for anyone who is attracted by the beauty that exists in simple knots.

A SHORT BACKGROUND

Macramé, like many another craft, suffered a loss of popularity for a time and became almost a lost art. When it was reintroduced

A Macramé wall hanging adds a decorative and exciting touch to what otherwise would be a dull corner.

(Facing page) Wall hanging, "Variations #5", 7¼" x 17½", worked in three colors—in black and white rug wool and brown 1½ lea linen.

towards the end of the Victorian period, people enthusiastically adopted it as a new craft, to such an extent that Sylvia was prompted to write in her book: "This kind of fancy-work is not exactly a novelty, except in the sense that when anything becomes so old as to be forgotten, its revival has all the effects of a first appearance." It was put to great use during this period, and elaborate fringes and tassels were produced in enormous quantities to trim curtains, mantelpieces, shelves, and four-poster beds. Sylvia even prompted her "fair reader . . . to work rich trimmings for black and coloured costumes, both for home wear, garden parties, seaside ramblings, and balls—fairylike adornments for household and underlinen. . . ."

The earliest form of Square Knot work is said to have originated in Arabia during the 13th century—Macramé comes from the Arabic *Migramah,* which means ornamental fringe and braid. The Spaniards, after learning the art from the Moors, spread it to southern Europe, possibly as early as the 14th century—certainly by the 16th, since its use is documented in a painting in Valladolid Cathedral, Spain.

Macramé was also popular in Italy around that time. In more recent days, however, in Turin, at an open-air school called Casa del Sole, young children—some five and six years old—became adept at doing a form of Macramé called the *Cavandoli Stitch.* This stitch, created by Mrs. Valentina Cavandoli to amuse and occupy the children in her care, is worked in two colors and is really another name for work produced by the Double Half Hitch. Some Cavandoli work is offered on pages 56–57.

France has produced a great deal of Macramé, and there is sufficient historical data to suggest that it was an established art in that country by the late 14th century. It is not known exactly when *Le Macramé,* by Thérèse de Dillmont, was written, or even when her *Encyclopedia on Needlework,* which contains a chapter on Macramé, was published, but I would venture to say that it was in the early 1800's. The examples in these books are extremely interesting and clearly exhibit the tremendous range of knotting possibilities.

Not to be overlooked is the contribution that seafaring men have made to Macramé. It cannot be said when they first began knotting to while away their long hours at sea, but as early as the 15th century they were using knotted articles for barter in India and China. Outstanding examples of sailors' work are to be found in the many maritime museums; two can be seen at the Seamen's Church Institute of New York City. These are large picture frames made with heavy seine twine, the traditional material used by maritime men.

Macramé is thought to have been introduced into England in the late 1600's by Queen Mary, wife of William of Orange, who learned the craft in Holland. During the time of George III, the knotting of

A charming example of Cavandoli work can be seen at the top of this Italian bag with Macramé fringe. Author's collection, gift from Donnie Mac Nab Brown.

(Above) American turn-of-the-century Macramé fringe for four-poster bed, approximately 18″ high. Collection of Cooper-Hewitt Museum of Design, Smithsonian Institute.

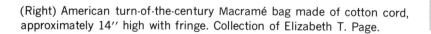

(Right) American turn-of-the-century Macramé bag made of cotton cord, approximately 14″ high with fringe. Collection of Elizabeth T. Page.

fringes was a great pastime; his wife, Queen Charlotte, in the 1780's was making Macramé fringe at court.

PROJECTS

Since there are so many items that can be knotted, and such a variety of knots to work them in, it might be difficult for the beginner to know where to start. I have therefore presented a cross section of items from the practical to the decorative. Seventeen projects are included, with complete directions and diagrams wherever necessary. In all instances, a handsome piece can be developed that will give pleasure in the making and in the using as well.

The intention of this book in giving directions is to build confidence so that each idea will be a springboard to your own creativity. Perhaps, after doing a few projects, you will want to try your own ideas, or perhaps you will want to vary a project by adding a knotting variation. By all means do so, and to aid you in this there is information on yarn, color, design, and texture. This information, together with the knowledge you will have gained from the explanatory text and the diagrams of the knots, should enable you to start on the road to designing your own pieces.

SAMPLERS

Making samplers of each knot, and in all its variations, will pay dividends in the understanding that you will soon have of the knotting process. Eventually, you will be able to tell how a piece of Macramé was knotted by just looking at it.

Until a complete knowledge of the knots is achieved, it is recommended that the beginner make samplers in one color—natural or white—since the knots will then be easier to see. Use as many variations on the knots as you wish. By using three different yarns, even greater interest is added. Experiment to your heart's content and then put what you have learned into a finished piece.

REFERENCES

At the conclusion of this book there is an index for quick reference, a list of suppliers of materials, a bibliography, and a list of book-dealers. Also listed are schools and workshops where courses in Macramé are offered periodically.

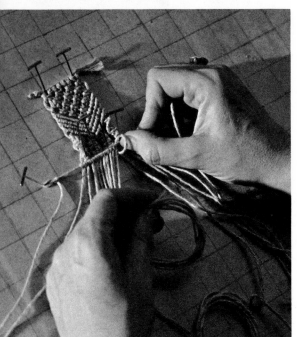

Method of working in Macramé on a knotting board, with the article placed and pinned against guidelines. Here a new cord is being added on with a row of Horizontal Double Half Hitches.

(Facing page) Detail of wall hanging, "Variations #11", 12" x 64", using natural 1½ lea linen and tan and dark green rug wool. Collection of W. Easton Pribble.

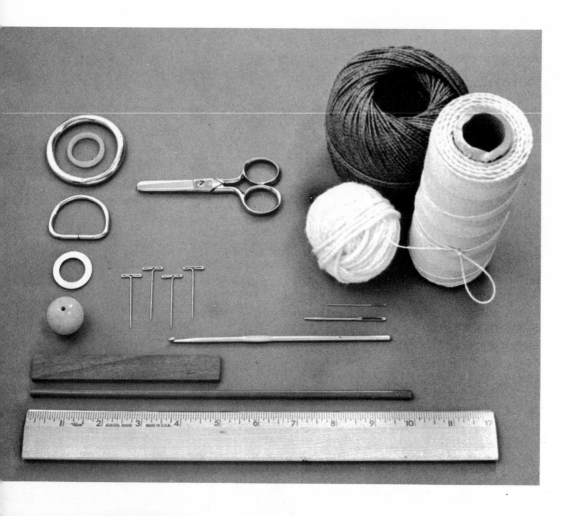

Scissors
"T" Pins
Yarns
Embroidery Needles
Crochet Hook
Woodstrips
Ruler
Beads and Rings
Knotting Board

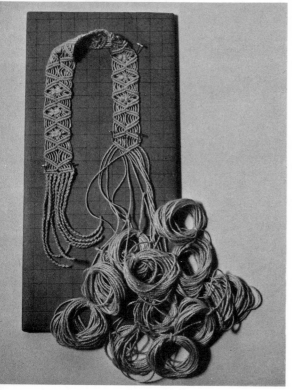

Equipment

The basic tools for Macramé work are simple and consist of scissors, "T" pins, and a knotting board. All other items are accessories or adornments. The embroidery needle and crochet hook are used occasionally for finishing off; chopsticks, hardwood, beads, rings, and loops for headings and decorations. Two metal loops make a belt buckle, as shown on pages 50–51.

THE KNOTTING BOARD

The knotting board is the working surface; the one shown is a piece of Celotex, an insulating material, covered with brown wrapping paper. Celotex can be cut into various sizes; a good selection to have would be sizes 12″ x 24″, 20″ x 36″, and 24″ x 48″, or whatever other size suits the piece you plan to make. In place of Celotex, padded cardboard may be used or cork covered with paper. The important thing is that the board be lightweight, rigid, yet pliable enough so that pins can be easily inserted.

YARNS

Yarns used for Macramé should be strong enough to withstand the abrasion that knotting produces and should not have a lot of give or elasticity. Smooth-surfaced yarns are best since they are the most satisfactory to work with and do not detract from the textural interest of the knots.

Knitting yarns are not desirable since they have too much elasticity, but some can be used once their limitations are understood and samplers have been made with them. Yarns used for Irish sweaters usually have less elasticity than do knitting worsteds and can be tested and considered for use in stoles and pillow covers.

The two hanging planters on page 31 were knotted with marline twine, obtained at marine supply stores. It is a fairly stiff material and so does not lend itself well to the Double Half Hitch Knot, but, since it does withstand the weather, I have used it to make outdoor hangings, such as shown on pages 34–35.

Jute is an effective material, not too costly, and the thickness of the yarn gives quick results. One word of caution, however: jute is not colorfast, so it is best not worked in colors if the piece is to be subjected to direct natural or electric light for any length of time. Seine twine, an old favorite of knotters, is excellent. It is stiffer than most twine but can be made pliable by rinsing in a fabric softener. Heavy rope, twine, and cord purchased in hardware stores can also be tried. Wool, linen, and silk are also excellent.

Linen has a wide latitude of colors and weights and is one of the most desirable of knotting yarns. It is one of my favorites because it has the strength and diversity of character that few other yarns offer. It combines well with wool and silk, as can be seen in the wall hangings shown in this book. Because of its fraying qualities, however, 1½ lea linen requires skill to use. Silk is not the easiest of yarns to obtain but is well worth the effort involved in finding it.

In many cases I have used fine linen and silk doubled, tripled and so on until I obtained the thickness necessary for the weight needed (as in Gazebo, pages 76–77). I have also combined two thicknesses of linen and one of rug wool for scale and texture, as in the black and white rug sample, page 57. This technique adds a new dimension to a piece and makes possible the use of yarns that could not be used to advantage singly.

Handspun yarns of quality lend themselves well to the more knowledgeable knotter. The Indians of Mitla, Mexico, who work beautifully in Macramé, do a great deal of their knotting in these yarns. Two examples of their work are shown on pages 44–45. Very heavy unspun roving provides scale and is interesting when combined with other yarns, as in Cascade, pages 72–73.

1. #1 Rattail rayon	9. Mexican ixtle
2. Silk cord	10. Jute-Tone
3. 1½ Lea linen	11. African sisal
4. 10/5 Linen	12. Leather lacing
5. 40/12 Linen cable	13. Avanti rug wool
6. 12/16 Linen cable	14. Pat rug wool
7. Linen cable	15. Wool roving
8. Marline twine	

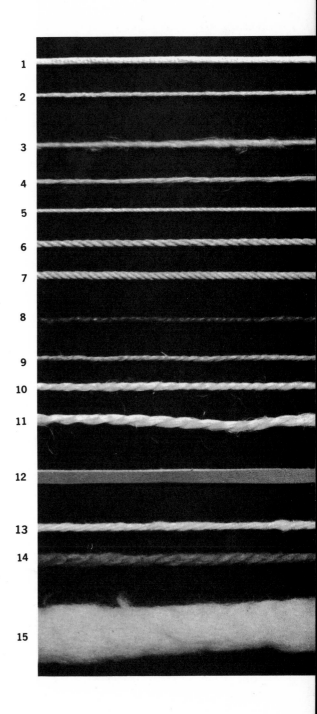

Project Previews

A few projects that appear in this book are shown on these two pages to introduce you to Macramé pieces that you can make. I have tried to present a varied arrangement throughout to suit different interests, tastes, and developments of skill.

In addition to the many pieces that I made for the projects—which include hanging planters, tote bag, placemat, wall hangings, purse, bracelets, room divider, pillow cover, and sashes and belts, plus ideas for others—I have also presented some of my wall hangings (an example is on the facing page), and have described them as to technique, knots, and materials used. This analysis was done not so that you could copy the individual pieces, but so that you would be better able to understand the progression of knots in their variations and how their combination can produce a work of art. Rugs and mats, also included as projects, are a relatively new departure for Macramé and one that I hope you will find exciting.

This combination of projects and analysis of technique offers the best way to begin your adventure into Macramé. While the pieces presented are all different, they have one thing in common—they are all made up of the two basic knots (the Half Hitch and the Half Knot) and their variations.

As you build up your skills and become more and more intrigued with the interplay of knotting patterns and yarn textures, new ideas and endless possibilities for further exploration will open up before you.

(Left) Hanging vase—see page 31.

(Below) Belt #2—see pages 50–51.

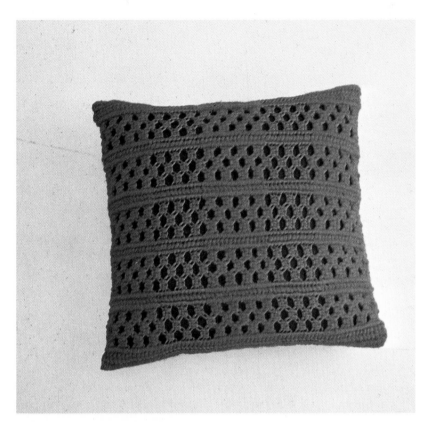

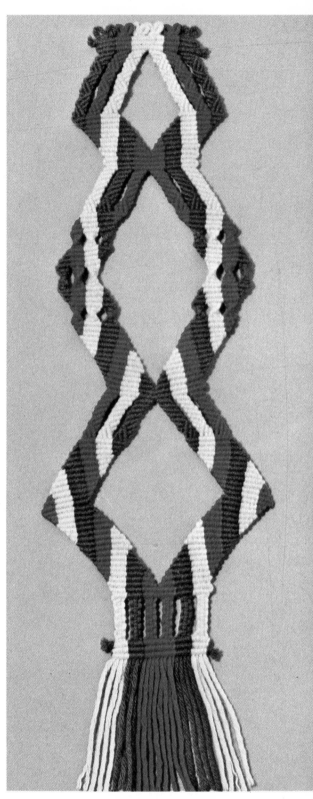

Pillow cover—see pages 42–43.

Blue and gold rug—see pages 52–53.

Wall hanging, Spirit of '76—see pages 60–61.

Preparing the Yarn

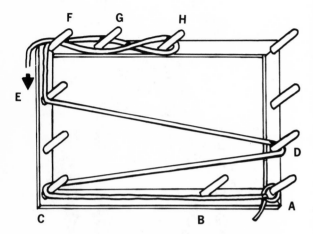

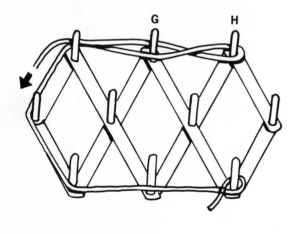

(Above) Ends being measured off on a warping board. Note the cross between G ahd H. (Below) Ends can also be measured off on an expanding hat rack.

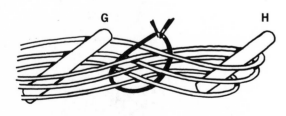

Close-up of cross, showing loose loop of contrasting yarn separating the ends.

The yarn is prepared for knotting by calculating the length of the ends and measuring off. An *end* is an individual length of yarn.

HOW TO CALCULATE

The ends should be 3½ to 4 times longer than the piece you plan to make, but since they are doubled in half for knotting, they are measured 7 to 8 times longer. For example, if the piece will have a finished length of 1 yd., measure each end to 7 or 8 yds. When each end is doubled for knotting, it will then be two ends, each 3½ to 4 yds. long. Measure ends generously and then add to them. This is no time to apply "Waste not, want not." It is better to have extra yarn than to run short and have to add at an inconvenient place in the design. If, however, you should be in this situation, see Splicing, page 25.

Making a Sampler. Heavy yarns take up more length in knotting than lightweight ones, so allow for this in the calculations. Make a sampler, at least 3″ x 6″, to gauge the length and to see how many ends will be needed for the width. To determine the number, tie four ends into a Square Knot (see pages 16–17) and measure the knot's width. If it is ½″, for example, you know you will need eight ends to the inch.

When you know what you want to make, or if you are searching for ideas, knot the yarn in several ways to know how it will tie and to gauge its texture and desirability. Keep notes of the amount used, its source, the number of ends and their length. Such records are valuable when planning future Macramé pieces.

MEASURING OFF ENDS

Warping Board. Once you know how long the ends should be, measure them off. This can be done with a ½ yd. x 1 yd. weaver's warping board. Begin by cutting one end, in a contrasting color, to the calculated length. Tie this measuring cord around peg A and wind it out to its full length as shown in the diagram. Making a cross between pegs G and H keeps the ends in order. With the measuring cord as guide, measure off the ends and cut them at peg A. In this way, ends may be removed in sections, and measurements will not be lost. To keep easier count of the ends, tie every group of ten with a loose loop of contrasting yarn.

Other Methods. If you don't have a warping board, C-clamps, or holding pegs, can be used. Attach clamps to opposite ends of a table and wind the yarn from peg to peg. Remember to make the cross. There is still another method. It takes longer, but it works. Measure the yarn against a yardstick, then cut it. Keeping this end as the measuring cord, measure off the needed number of ends.

MOUNTING ENDS

Knotting Board. The board is covered with brown wrapping paper, which affords good contrast to the yarns. To ready the board, pull the paper tightly, tape it on the reverse side, and mark it off into 1″ squares. These guidelines will help you knot to the proper length and width. Work at the board in the way most comfortable for you —I usually sit with the board leaning against a table edge and resting in my lap. A convenient point to begin the work is usually the middle of the board, or about 10″ from the bottom. As knotting progresses, move the work upward.

Holding Cord. The ends are knotted onto a holding cord (a horizontal length) with the Reversed Double Half Hitch Knot (see diagram; also page 17) or onto a chopstick, ring, bracelet or whatever you feel suits the piece. They can also be looped around "T" pins.

Tie an Overhand Knot onto each side of the holding cord and pin securely to the knotting board. The cord must be kept taut. At times it is also used as a knot-bearing cord (over which knots are tied); in that case, make an Overhand Knot on one side only, preferably the left.

As each end is knotted onto the holding cord, pin it to the board. Move pins down constantly as the work progresses. They should never be more than an inch from the working area and can even be just in the row above. Slant pins away from you, and *anchor them firmly.* If the design should become irregular, either the pinning is not sufficient or some knots are being tied too tightly.

WINDING ENDS

When ends are too long to handle conveniently, their lengths can be reduced by making hand bobbins or butterflies (see diagrams), or by using rubber bands. Each end is wound separately.

KNOTS

Only two elementary knots are essential to Macramé—the Half Knot, also called the Macramé Knot, and the Half Hitch. There are various combinations of these knots, some distinctive enough to have their own names. Different texts refer to them under different names but, once seen, they can be recognized as old friends.

Knots can be easily learned from the diagrams in this book. In addition to those in the section on Knots which follows, others are included in the book where they apply. Practice them by making samplers, using different yarns and doubling the number of ends. Make the knots in light-colored yarns so that they will be easier to see.

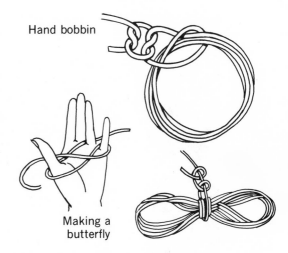

Hand bobbin

Making a butterfly

Hand Bobbin: Wind the ends in circles around the fingers and fasten with a Square Knot when ends reach about 18″ from holding cord.

Butterfly: Clasp loose end of yarn and wind length in figure 8's as shown.

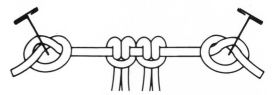

Two Reversed Double Half Hitches shown mounted on a holding cord. The two Overhand Knots on either side are pinned securely to the knotting board.

THINGS TO REMEMBER

Keep the holding cord in a steady position when mounting ends.

Keep the knot-bearing cord motionless and taut when in use.

Tie every knot close to the previous knot unless the design directs otherwise.

Keep ends straight, in order, and not twisted, particularly when knots are being made over them.

Ends are always doubled in half before knotting begins. When the number of cut ends is given in the projects, this always refers to measured-off ends and not to doubled ends.

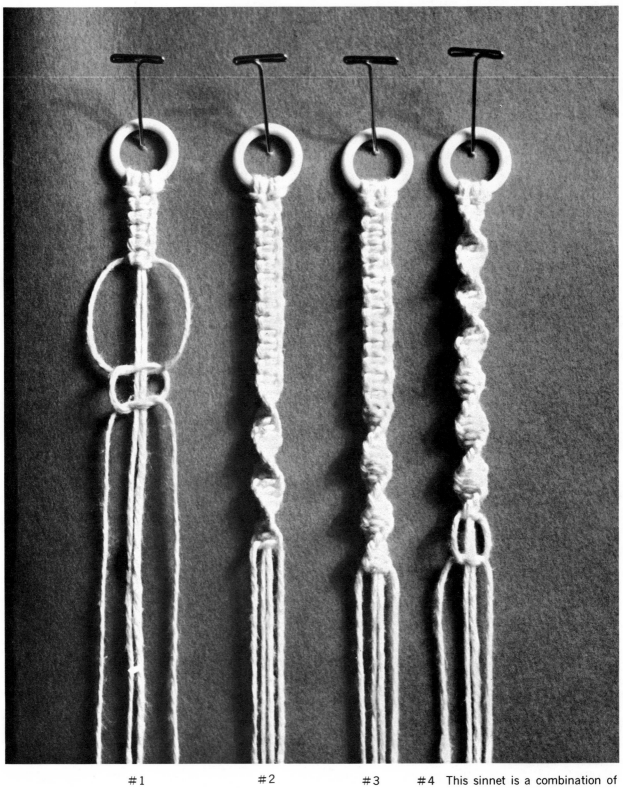

#1   #2   #3   #4 This sinnet is a combination of left-right, right-left Half Knots.

The Square Knot and The Half Knot

The Square Knot is made up of two Half Knots, one going to the left, the other to the right. Four ends are used; the center two, known as fillers or core ends, are held taut until the knot is completed. As you practice you will be making sinnets (braided cordage), as seen on the facing page. The knotting patterns below correspond by number with those used in the sinnets illustrated. In Sinnet #1 the knotting pattern consists of a series of Square Knots. In Sinnets #2 and #3, using a Square Knot and a Reversed Square Knot respectively, a twist effect is obtained in the lower sections by repeating the Half Knot. Sinnet #4 is a combination of the lower sections of Sinnets #2 and #3. In Sinnets #1 and #4 the last knot is shown in construction.

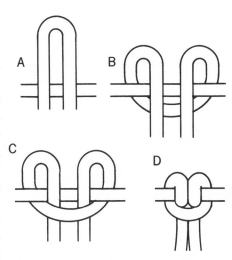

How to mount ends on holding cord with Reversed Double Half Hitches.

TO MAKE SINNETS ON FACING PAGE:

#1 Square Knot	#2 Square Knot with Half Knot twist	#3 Reversed Square Knot with Half Knot twist

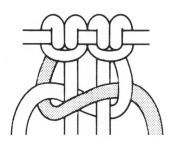

Half Knot, left-right

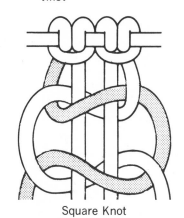

Square Knot

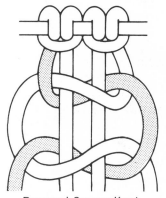

Reversed Square Knot

Square Knot, left-right, right-left, completed. Continue with series of Square Knots.

Continue Half Knot, left-right, to make twist.

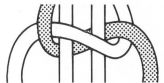

Continue Half Knot, right-left, to make twist.

Square Knot sinnet of leather made into handles adds new interest to old bureau drawers.

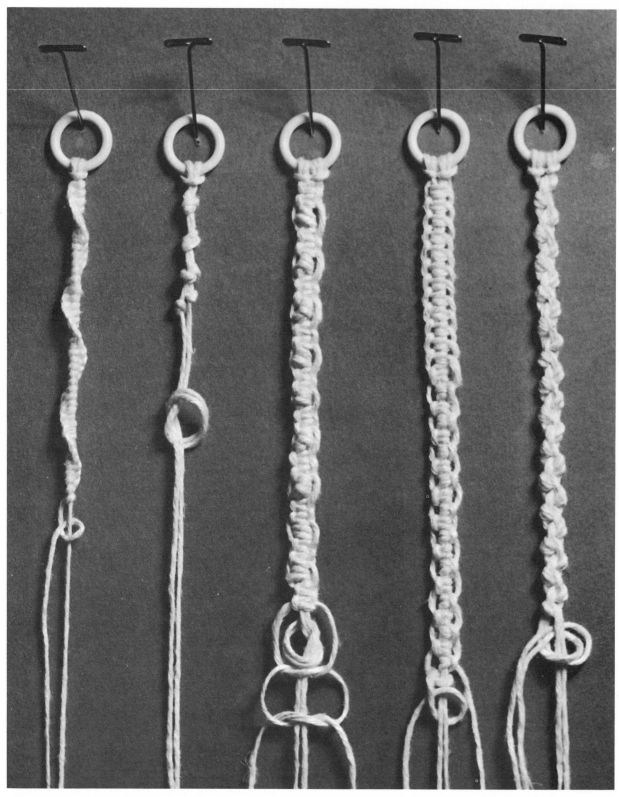

#5   #6   #7   #8   #9

The Half Hitch, The Overhand Knot

The Half Hitch is the most practical knot in Macramé since a number of variations may be obtained from it. The Overhand Knot is tied in a way somewhat similar to the Half Hitch but is applied differently. A series of Overhand Knots using either a single end or multiends creates texture. It also can be used to end a sinnet. In diagram #7, it is used between Square Knots for added interest.

The Double Chain Knot can be made with two ends or multiends. Using it in two colors with a heavy yarn makes an interesting sash.

The construction of all these knots can be easily followed from the diagrams. In each case the knotting patterns correspond by number with those used in the sinnets on the facing page.

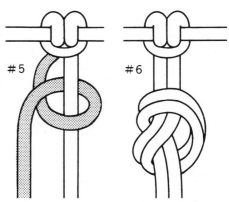

#5 Half Hitch Knot
Continue for sinnet.

#6 Overhand Knot, two ends
Continue for sinnet.

TO MAKE SINNETS ON FACING PAGE:

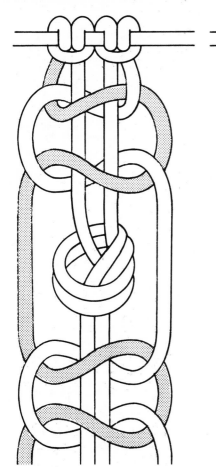

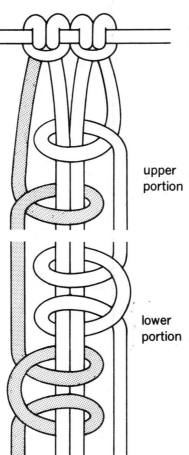

upper portion

lower portion

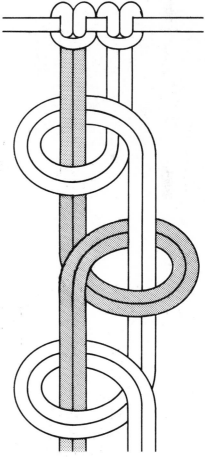

#7 Square Knot with Overhand Knot on core ends

#8 Alternating Half Hitches and Reversed Double Half Hitches

#9 Double Chain Knot with four ends

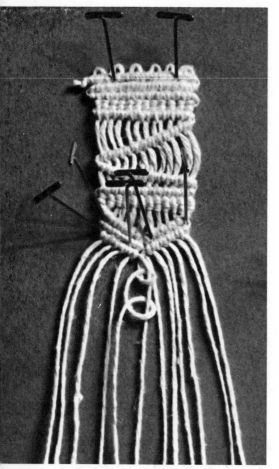

Sampler showing Horizontal, Vertical, and Diagonal Double Half Hitches.

The Double Half Hitch

It would be difficult to say which of the Double Half Hitch variations gives the most exciting results. They are certainly all distinctive. This book contains several projects that well illustrate the endless possibilities of this important and versatile knot. Three versions are diagrammed here—the Horizontal, Vertical, and Diagonal. Each end goes over the knot-bearing cord twice while completing the row (making two Half Hitches). Keep the knot-bearer secure across each row and held sharply in the determined direction. Draw up knots closely and pin each row after completion. The knot-bearer must be measured off longer than other ends.

TO MAKE HORIZONTAL ROWS:

A End #1 is knot-bearer.

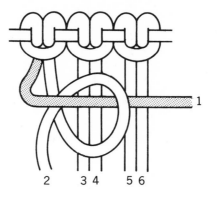

B With end #2, make Double Half Hitch.

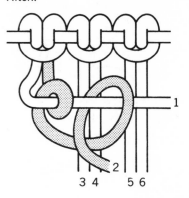

C Repeat for end #3.

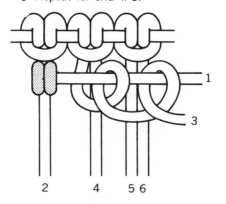

D Complete row and return.

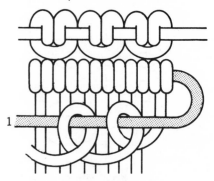

TO MAKE VERTICAL ROWS:

A Start   **B** Continue   **C** Return

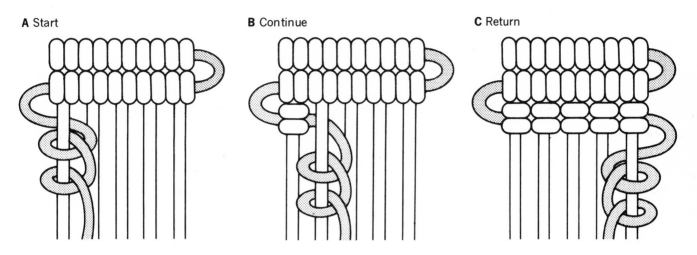

TO MAKE DIAGONAL ROWS:

A End #1 is knot-bearer.   **B** With each end, make Double Half Hitch.   **C** Start 2nd row with end #2 as knot-bearer.

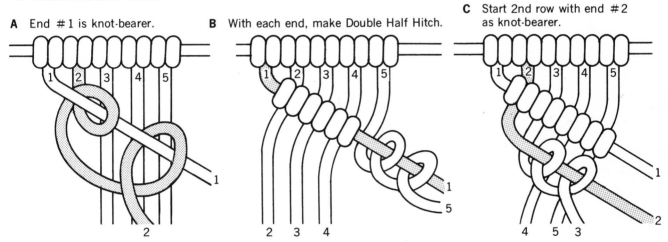

D Method of crossing ends when diagonal rows meet.   **E** To create open spaces, diagonal rows are not crossed.

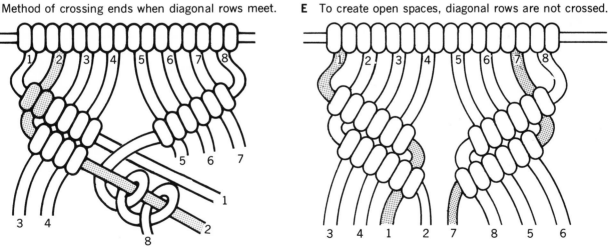

Continue by making a row of knots with end #7, then tie it over end #1.

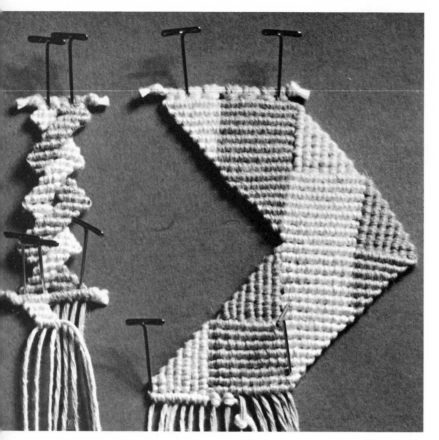

Sampler #1   Sampler #2

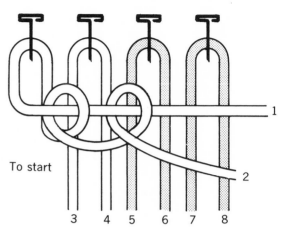

To start

To start, loop ends around "T" pins and begin 1st row of Horizontal Double Half Hitches

FACING PAGE:

A, B, C Start angling technique, working from left to right.

D To continue, end #5 is brought to horizontal position and Horizontal Double Half Hitches start with end #6.

AA To reverse angling pattern direction.

BB To vary color pattern.

Double Half Hitch (Angling Technique)

The Horizontal and Vertical Double Half Hitches can be varied in an angling technique which makes color changes possible, as well as the creating of pointed areas for profile shaping.

Sampler #1 consists of two angled sections made independently with Horizontal Double Half Hitches. The yarn is knotted from right to left for the first section and then from left to right. This alternating is continued until the desired length is reached. The second section is done in the same way, but the knotting starts from left to right. When both sections are the same length, they are interlocked simply by being placed together and secured with a row of Horizontal Double Half Hitches on a holding cord.

Sampler #2 consists of interknotting of colors by the angling technique. One by one ends are worked across in rows of Horizontal Double Half Hitches and are left on the right side. After a number of ends have been done, they are brought straight down and are used as knot-bearing cords for Vertical Double Half Hitches. The diagrams demonstrate the technique used.

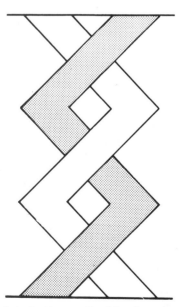

Interlocking method for Sampler #1

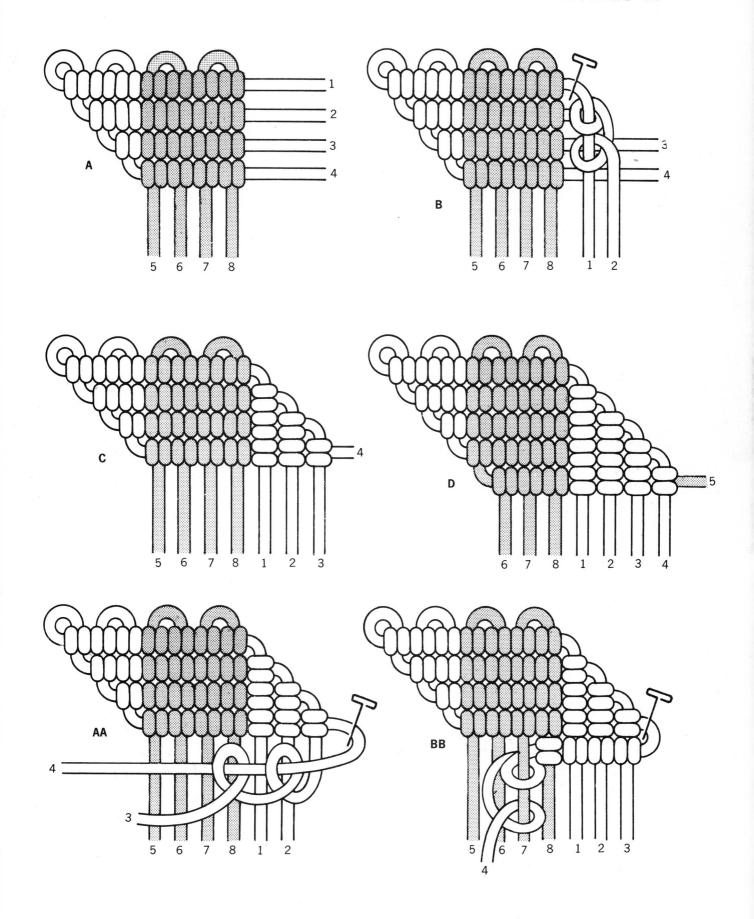

Headings and Picots

There are various ways of mounting ends onto a holding cord and some are very decorative.

The picots shown here are looped knots used to give variation to edge headings and other areas where a lacy effect is desired. Note the Hanging Vase on page 31.

#1   #2   #3

#1 Reversed Double
Half Hitch

#2 Double
Half Hitch

#3 Double Half
Hitch with Picot

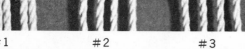

#4   #5   #6

#4, #5 Square Knot and
Square Knot with Picots

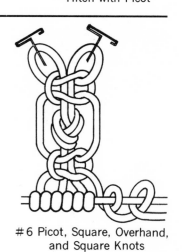

#6 Picot, Square, Overhand,
and Square Knots

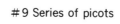

#7   #8   #9

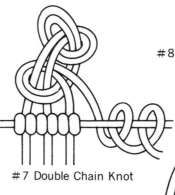

#8 Picot, Reversed
Double Half Hitch

#7 Double Chain Knot

#9 Series of picots

Finishing

For finishing off a piece, the remaining ends can be worked into a decorative fringe, or formed into sinnets, or they can be neatly trimmed, making a simple fringed edge. A Gathering Knot can be made (see diagram), using as many ends as you want. Tie it tightly so that it will hold and give a crisp look to the work. The ends can also be woven into the reverse side with an embroidery needle or crochet hook. Still another way is to set in a holding cord and mount a single row of Double Half Hitches, followed by a Square Knot and sinnets ending with a Gathering Knot. These and other ways of ending pieces will be found in the projects.

Decorative Edgings. Square Knots with multiends and Overhand Knots can be used to make decorative edges on draperies or tablecloths. The same idea can also be added to a sash, or to a knitted stole or afghan.

The curtain fringe in burlap on the right was started by pulling out about 12″ of the horizontal threads; Square Knots using twelve ends were then made. The directions are as follows:

    1st row—Square Knot 4,4,4 (4 ends on each side are tied over 4 ends)
    2nd row—Square Knot 2,8,2 (2 ends on each side are tied over 8 ends)
    3rd row—Square Knot 4,4,4
    4th row—Square Knot 2,8,2
    5th row—Overhand Knot with the center 8 ends.
    6th and 7th rows—Square Knots 2,4,2, using the 8 ends.
    8th row—Overhand Knot with the center 8 ends.
    9th row—Square Knot 4,4,4
    To Finish: Make a Gathering Knot and trim ends neatly.

splicing

At times ends must be replaced because their lengths were underestimated or they were pulled so tightly they snapped. In those instances splicing can be done. If the end breaks in a row of Double Half Hitches, overlap the broken ends and continue knotting the row, working them in (see diagram). Pull the exposed ends to the reverse side of the piece. For splicing at core of Square Knot, see diagram. When working on a large piece it is better to splice than to work with overly large butterflies. (See Blue & Gold rug, pages 52–53.)

switching ends

If you find on beginning a Square Knot sinnet, that the outside ends are much shorter than the core ends, switch them so that the core ends are on the outside. In this way you will not have to splice.

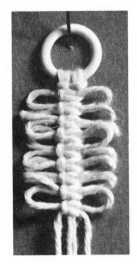

#10 Picot with Square Knots

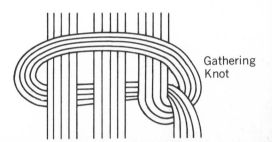

Gathering Knot

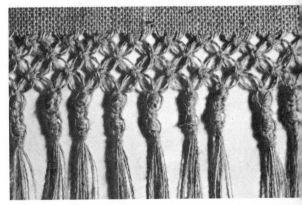

Curtain fringe in burlap.

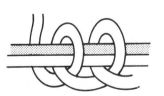

Splicing method for Double Half Hitch

Splicing method for Square Knot

Texture

The beauty of a Macramé piece is contained in the movement of the knots. The way they are arranged in a knotting pattern and the yarns that are chosen to work them combine to create a wealth of textural variations. Here are some examples, including several taken from pieces in this book.

COMBINING TEXTURES

The wall hanging to the left illustrates how a variety of materials can be harmoniously blended to create a unity in design and a richness of texture. A silver metal earring for mounting the work, wooden beads set in among knots, bobbles (see page 49) for raised areas, and two types of yarns in muted colors are all carefully balanced in a construction containing solid areas and open spaces. Added to these elements are the knotting patterns of the Double Half Hitch and Square Knot, which give direction and increased interest to the work.

OPEN SPACES WITH LINEAR KNOTTING DESIGN

On the upper right is a detail of a Mexican stole. The emphasis in this piece is on the unevenness of the handspun wool yarn that was used, and the way in which the unknotted areas seem to be loosely held together by a linear pattern of Half Knots. The open textural effect is that of an airy fabric, soft and pliable to the touch, yet it has bulk and is actually very sturdy. It is an ideal apparel texture.

CLOSE KNOTTING WITH RUG WOOL YARN

The detail in the center of a blue and gold rug is an example of how compactness in design can create texture. This strong, even-surfaced fabric was achieved by close knotting of the Double Half Hitch worked horizontally and vertically. Rug yarn is used throughout to produce a thick pile and the firmness necessary for its intended use.

COMBINING CONTRASTING YARNS

The detail at lower right of the wall hanging Cascade exhibits yet another textural quality. This one shows the distinctly different effect achieved when contrasting yarns are combined. Here an unspun thick wool roving and a linen cable are used. The result of their constant interplay becomes the dominant feature in this work, created mainly with the Square Knot.

(Facing Page) Detail of wall hanging, Misterio, shows a variety of materials combined. Collection of Anne Stackhouse.

Detail of Mexican stole—see also pages 44–45.

Detail of blue and gold rug—see also pages 52–53.

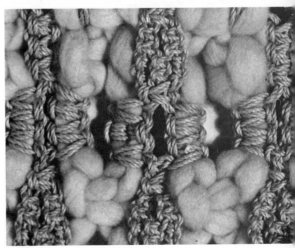

Detail of wall hanging, Cascade—see pages 72–73.

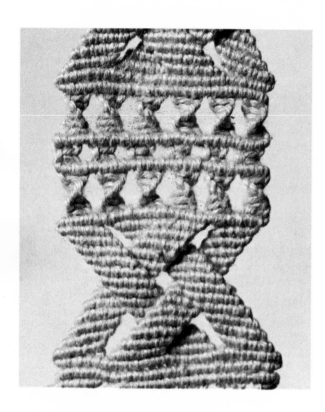

(Top) Detail of wall hanging, Peking—see also pages 64–65.

(Right) Detail of multicolor sash—see also pages 48–49.

(Below) Detail of back of red pillow cover—see also pages 42–43.

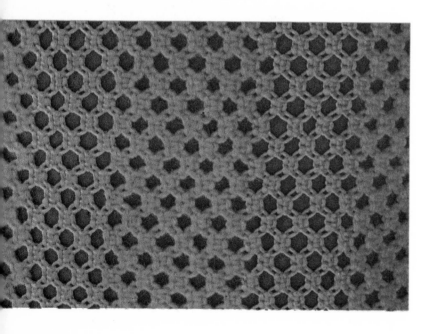

Color and Design

Although color is so personal to each of us and our own reactions to it vary as do our moods, there are nevertheless several color considerations to keep in mind when planning a piece of Macramé. Remember that the beauty of this craft is in its knotting and the way it is arranged in patterns. However, if you have an interesting design in mind, and you want to use color, or if you desire a particular color accent in a room, by all means plan the Macramé piece in the color or colors of your choosing; but it would then be best to keep the construction of the knotting simple.

One way to test what happens to color in a design is to make samplers using different-textured materials and a variety of knots.

INTRICATE PATTERN, USING ONE COLOR

When a piece is planned to combine different textures, an intricate knotting pattern, and added elements of design, color is best used singly. Note the detail of Peking (facing page, top left), in which some of the knotting variations can be seen. The color matches and blends with the beads that are incorporated as part of the design. The sparkle of the beads and their color variations need no further color contrast to offset them.

TWO YARNS OF THE SAME COLOR

Using closely related values of one color can give more interest and depth to the finished piece. The detail of the red pillow (facing page, lower left) is an example of how two different yarns of the same color can work to enhance each other. The elegant sheen of the red rayon is well complemented by the quiet mat finish of the red wool. Another dimension of contrast is added where two yarns meet in areas of Square Knots. The knotting pattern is kept simple.

STRONG COLOR CONTRAST

In the detail of the sash (facing page, right), multicolor ends of two different yarns are knotted into a repeat diagonal design. Three dramatic colors can be successfully combined because the knotting pattern is a subtle one. The piece is worked periodically from the back, thus changing the character of the surface and contributing an added textural element. Bobbles are another design interest.

ONE COLOR WITH CONTRASTING BEADS

Color contrast is also achieved by varying the density of the knotted areas. The detail of Nightbird (right) shows a knotting pattern sufficiently interesting to require only white wooden beads for contrast. These beads serve to unify the open spaces and dense areas in the pattern. They also accent the outline of the triangular shape.

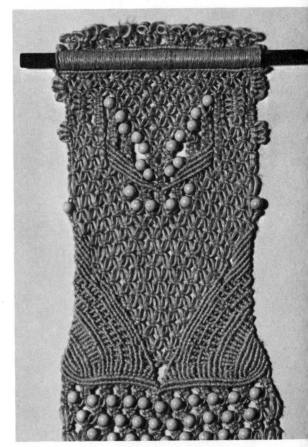

Detail of wall hanging, Nightbird—see also pages 74–75.

Hanging planter made with
Double Chain Knot sinnets.

Hanging Planters

The three projects shown here use simple sinnets and few knots. They are designed to help you create charming and useful pieces by combining yarn and found objects. **Note:** The general rule that ends should measure 3½ to 4 times the finished length of the piece does not apply to the weed pot or hanging vase. Since there are so few knots to tie in these pieces, less yarn is taken up.

Remember, ends are always doubled before knotting begins.

hanging planter

Size: 20″ long

Materials: 10/5 linen. Natural. Frederick J. Fawcett, Inc. The planter is an old insulating cap from a telephone pole.

Knot: Double Chain (use 4 ends as 2—see pages 18–19).

Cut Ends: 2 ends, each 6½ yds. long. 4 ends, each 4¾ yds. long.

Directions: Pin the two 6½-yd.-long ends to the board, leaving a small loop at the top. Tie a sinnet of Double Chain Knots. Attach finished sinnet around container by pulling the ends through the loop.

Mount the remaining four ends onto the finished sinnet at intervals of one third. Make two Double Chain Knot sinnets where you have attached the ends.

To Finish: Tie the three sinnets together with an Overhand Knot. Trim excess as desired.

charlie brown's weed pot

Materials: Marline twine. Any cylindrical- or conical-shaped container. A disk with four holes or a ring is used for the base.

Knots: Square, Reversed Double Half Hitch, Overhand.

Cut Ends: 8 ends, each 2¾ yds. long.

Directions: See facing page.

To Finish: Tie the ends together with an Overhand Knot and trim.

hanging vase

Materials: Marline twine. The container is a triangular jam jar.

Knots: Square, Overhand, Picot.

Cut Ends: 6 ends, each 3 yds. long.

Directions: See facing page.

To Finish: About 28″ from the last knot, gather the ends together and make an Overhand Knot by which to hang the piece.

Weed pot with Square Knots alternating. Pottery by Charlie Brown.

To Start Base

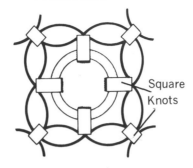

Square Knots

Directions, Weed Pot. Into each hole of the base, or at four places on a ring, mount two ends, using the Reversed Double Half Hitch. This gives four ends from each hole. Make a Square Knot with each four ends. Take two ends from each knot; leave 1¼″ space. Tie a Square Knot, Overhand Knot, and Square Knot. Take two ends from each knot; leave 2″ space. Tie a Double Square Knot at each corner. With outside ends of each Square Knot, tie an Overhand Knot with four ends.

To Start Base

Directions, Hanging Vase. Intertwine four ends with the loop ends. With each four ends, make a sinnet of 5 Square Knots. *Take the two outside ends and leave 1″ space. Make an Overhand Knot. Bring one core end each from 2 Square Knots and make a Square Knot below the Overhand Knot. Next make 3 Picot Knots (page 24), ending with 1 Square Knot *. Repeat * to * with the other ends. Take two ends from each knot, leave 2″ space, and tie an Overhand Knot with four ends. Do 2 more such knots with the other ends.

Hanging vase with picots.

Working two sides of tote bag.

The finished bag.

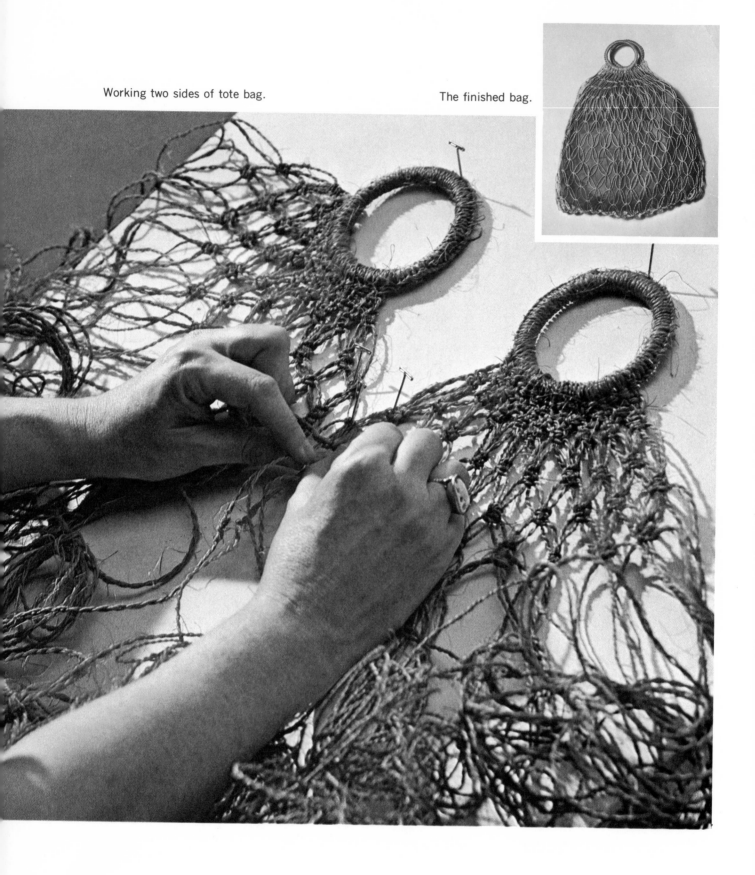

Tote Bag

This project results in a handy and attractive piece and serves to introduce the Square Knot used double and in an alternating technique. It is important here that the knots be kept evenly spaced.

Size: 15″ wide at the center, 25″ long, including bracelets and fringe.

Materials: Mexican ixtle. Pink and green. This tying cord is available where gift wrappings are sold.
Two bracelets. If you can get matching colored bracelets, do so; then they will not have to be covered with knots.

Knots: Half Hitch, Reversed Double Half Hitch, Square and Double Square in alternating rows.

Cut Ends: Pink—18 ends, each 4 yds. long.
Green—18 ends, each 4 yds. long.
2 extra ends, one of each color, 1 yd. long each, to cover bracelets.

Note: Use a long narrow knotting board since it will be inserted between the two sides of the piece. As you make each knot, dampen it with wet fingertips. Don't get knots too wet or the yarn fibers will separate.

To Begin: Partially cover one bracelet with pink yarn, using the Half Hitch. Attach 10 ends (that is, 5 doubled) of pink with the Reversed Double Half Hitch. Attach 16 ends (8 doubled) of green in the same manner. Attach 10 more ends of pink in the same manner. Fill up remaining spaces with Half Hitches in pink. Repeat with second bracelet except reverse the color order.

Directions: Work each side as follows: 2 rows of Square Knots alternating. Knot them close together. 1 row of Double Square Knots alternating (see lower diagram). Leave ¾″ space and do a 2nd row of Double Square Knots alternating. Leave 1″ space and do a 3rd row of Double Square Knots alternating.

Pin the two sides next to each other and on each side do 3 more rows of Double Square Knots alternating.

Now join the sides together, as shown in the photograph, using the edge of the knotting board. From this point on the piece lies on both sides of the board. Continue knotting to the length of the bag.

To Finish: When you have worked all the knots down to the same point, match the two sides knot for knot. Tie bundles of 8 ends together, using an Overhand Knot and leave a couple of inches hanging. Or turn the bag inside out, tie an Overhand Knot on the inside, and trim excess close to the knot.

Making Half Hitches on bracelet for handles.

Knotting Pattern:

Double Square Knots in alternate rows.

Joining the two sides on edge of knotting board.

Patio Hangings

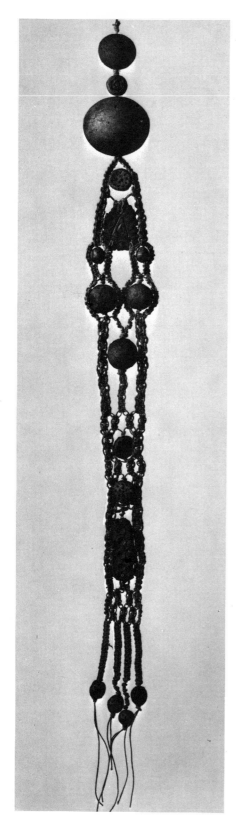

Simple sinnets move into a new dimension when they are used in multiples, and there is increased textural interest when they are combined with other materials.

The two hanging pieces shown on this and on the facing page combine Macramé with raku pottery pieces, and are examples of how one craftsman's work can enhance and support another's. These constructions were done for a craft exhibit that my friend Charlie Brown and I had at the Signature Shop in Atlanta, Ga.

Charlie Brown, well-known potter from Mandarin, Florida, had sent me an assortment of raku beads, balls, and disks to incorporate with Macramé. The considerations in planning these pieces were proper balance and distribution of the raku, always keeping in mind the textural quality of their surface enrichment and the difference in their sizes. A heavy yarn was called for, a dark-colored one, to complement the smoky shadings of the fired pieces. Marline twine was used both for its texture and color and for its durability.

There were certain limitations to be faced in planning the designs due to the uneven distribution of the raku pieces I had available. For the patio hanging on the facing page, I selected nine beads of one size, seven beads of another, three lozenge-shaped beads, one odd bead, and one disk.

The layout of the beads indicated using an odd number of them across the top and then working several rows before adding two beads in the center with the disk placed evenly beneath them. From this point on, the working areas were divided into three parts, using the remaining beads in the manner shown. The piece is composed of sinnets made up primarily of three knots—Square, Overhand, and Reversed Half Hitch.

The second piece (left), although similarly planned, was not made as a wall hanging but as a free-hanging suspended form.

Once again with an odd number of raku pieces, I built a design. The largest two of the beads were chosen to head the piece, with a small flat disk placed between them, and the knotting began from this point. Additional ends of marline twine were added on in several places in order to develop the width dictated by the placement of the beads. This piece was made up of simple sinnets using Square Knots and Overhand Knots.

(Left and facing page) Multisinnets combined with raku beads and disks were used to make these two patio hangings. Collection of Signature Shop, Atlanta, Ga. Raku pieces by Charlie Brown.

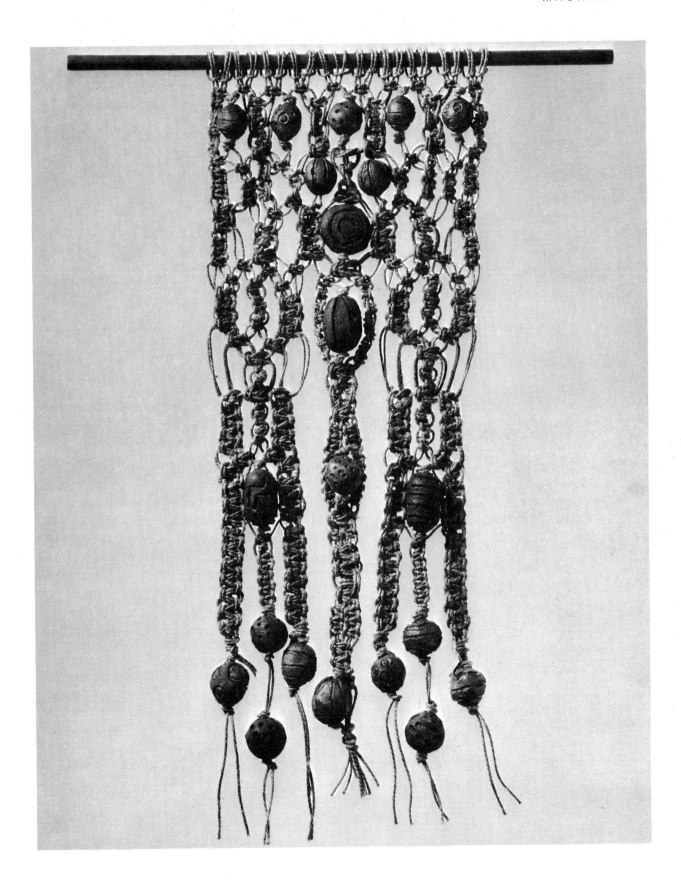

Knotting Pattern: Square Knot alternating.

Detail of starting point, upper left corner, showing variation of knots used.

Placemat

The Square Knot used in alternating rows is the featured knot in this project, as it was in the Tote Bag (see pages 32–33), but here it is more closely tied, giving a totally different effect. The knot-bearing cord, worked into the edge Square Knots so that no loose ends will be exposed, is an example of how to do an expert job, and also one of fine craftsmanship.

Size: 13″ x 20″

Material: 10/5 linen. Orange. Frederick J. Fawcett. Inc.

Knots: Square Knot and Double Half Hitch.

Cut Ends: 52 ends, each 5 yds. 20″ long.

Holding Cord: 4 yds.

Note: The holding cord is also the knot-bearing cord and is incorporated into the edge Square Knot after being used for a row of Horizontal Double Half Hitches, and all along the edge until needed again as a knot-bearing cord for the next row of Horizontal Double Half Hitches. This will give three core ends, as shown in the diagram on the facing page.

To Begin: Tie an Overhand Knot about an inch in on the holding cord. Pin the knot securely to the board just before the beginning of an inch square and on a horizontal guideline. Using all the ends, do 1 row of Horizontal Double Half Hitches (#2 Heading, page 24). Return and do another row of Horizontal Double Half Hitches.

Directions:
1 row, Double Square Knots
1 row, Horizontal Double Half Hitches
3 rows, Square Knots alternating
1 row, Horizontal Double Half Hitches
1 row, Triple Square Knots (sinnets)
1 row, Horizontal Double Half Hitches
5 rows, Square Knots alternating
1 row, Horizontal Double Half Hitches
*7 rows, Square Knots alternating
1 row, Horizontal Double Half Hitches*
Repeat * to * seven times.
1 row, Horizontal Double Half Hitches
5 rows, Square Knots alternating
1 row, Horizontal Double Half Hitches
3 rows, Square Knots

1 row, Horizontal Double Half Hitches
3 rows, Square Knots alternating
1 row, Horizontal Double Half Hitches
2 rows, Square Knots
2 rows, Horizontal Double Half Hitches

To Finish: With an embroidery needle or crochet hook, weave in the ends on the back side for at least ½". Trim.

If the mat does not lay flat, pin it to size on the knotting board every half inch. Spray lightly with water and allow it to dry.

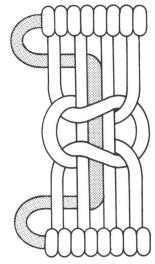

Square Knot with three core ends. Third end is knot-bearer and is worked into edge Square Knot until needed again.

Orange placemat, 13" x 20".

Bracelets and Beads

Most of us have items around the house such as beads, buttons with shanks, and interesting belt buckles that have been stored safely away in boxes or jars. Such found objects can be combined effectively with Macramé. A few ideas are presented here.

bracelets

For holiday wear or gift-giving, here is a simple way to get new bracelets out of old ones.

Materials: #1 Rattail. Red, grey, dark green. Fibre Yarn Co.
   Two bracelets, two bells

Knots: Square Knot and Reversed Double Half Hitch.

Cut Ends: Red and green—1 end each, 3½ yds. long.
   Grey—2 ends, 3½ yds. long.

Directions for Red and Grey Bracelet: Hold edge of bracelet towards you and attach the red yarn with Reversed Double Half Hitches so

Assortment of beads, buckles, bells, bracelets, and rings for use in Macramé pieces.

that the ends come on the left side. Attach the grey in the same manner, except have the ends come on the right side.

The bracelet is now used as the core for the Square Knot. Make tight Square Knots around the bracelet until it is covered. Pull the ends through the beginning knots with a needle and hide them behind several knots before trimming ends.

Directions for Green and Grey Bracelet: Start as above, attaching green and grey ends to bracelet. With Reversed Double Half Hitches, alternate colors until bracelet is covered. Attach bells to the green and grey ends before tucking the ends in and trimming off.

neckpiece

This idea for **a neckpiece** is a unique and attractive way to use beads from that broken necklace. You could also make a beaded sash or bracelet. Buttons with shanks can be used in the same manner.

Materials are 10/5 linen and beads of two sizes. The small beads were put onto a holding cord and alternated with Reversed Double Half Hitches. The piece consists of beads of two sizes, Square and Overhand Knots and a combination of the two, and Half Knots.

Adding on Beads: If you are adding wooden beads and the holes are too small for the ends to go through, use a rattail file to enlarge them. Apply fixative to ends to help pass them through the holes.

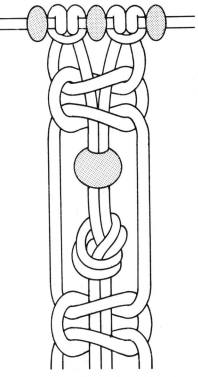

One way of arranging beads.

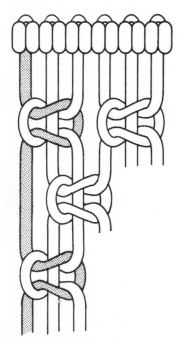

Knotting pattern

Hand bobbins shown on the piece being worked.

Room Divider

Two versions of the Square Knot are used here, one with a multiple of three double ends, the other using four double ends. Either version, used separately or in combination, creates a unique and interesting pattern. The dimensions for the room divider are given as 20″ x 60″, but of course alter them to whatever size you need. You may also wish to use a different yarn; jute would be very effective.

Size: 20″ x 60″

Materials: 10/5 linen. Natural and black. Frederick J. Fawcett, Inc.
The yarn is used double.
26″ black dowel

Knots: Square Knot and Horizontal Double Half Hitch.

Cut Ends: Natural—54 ends, each 9 yds. long.
Black—48 ends, each 9 yds. long.

Knot-bearing Cord: For each row of Horizontal Double Half Hitches, cut two ends, each 26″ long.

Note: The Square Knots are made with three ends doubled as shown in the diagram. Always start these knots on the left side. Reverse direction of each row of Horizontal Double Half Hitches; that is, if 1st row began on left side, start next row on right side.

To Begin: Tie a row of Reversed Double Half Hitches onto the dowel. Make a row of Horizontal Double Half Hitches on the knot-bearing cord, using doubled ends.

Directions:
*1. Do 1 row Square Knots.
2. Drop first end on left, and do 1 row Square Knots* There will be two free ends at end of row.
Repeat * to * 5 times, ending with row 1.
Do 1 row Horizontal Double Half Hitches, 1 row Square Knots, 1 row Horizontal Double Half Hitches
Repeat * to * 10 times, ending with row 1.
Repeat # to #
Repeat * to * 10 times, ending with row 1.
For a more open effect, one with more scale, make the Square Knots with four ends used as one.

To Finish: Individual taste is best here. Suggestions include trimming ends off neatly for a fringe effect, or making individual sinnets.

A dowel can also be used at the bottom, as it was at the top, particularly if you want the piece to remain taut in the width.

(Facing page) Room divider showing two Square Knot versions. The more closed pattern (top section) uses three doubled ends as one; the more open pattern (lower section) uses four doubled ends as one.

Knotting pattern: Double Square Knot alternating.

Pillow Cover

There are two interesting features to this project. One is the pattern created by the Square Knot in alternating rows; the other is the use of two yarns that are closely related in color but contrast greatly in texture. Two patterns are offered and can be used for back and front of the same pillow cover or for separate pillow covers.

Size: 10" x 10"

Materials: Avanti rug wool. Red. Craft Yarns of Rhode Island, Inc.
    #1 Rattail rayon. Red. Fibre Yarn Co.

Knots: Square Knot and Horizontal Double Half Hitch.

Cut Ends: Rug wool—24 ends, each 2 yds. 16" long.
    Rattail—12 ends, each 2 yds. 21" long.

Holding Cord: Used also as knot-bearing cord.
    Cut 6 yds of rug wool.

Note: All Square Knots are double in this piece.
    Arrange the ends as follows before beginning to knot: 16 wool, 12 rattail, 16 wool, 12 rattail, 16 wool.

Directions:
    For one side of pillow cover:
*Do 2 rows Horizontal Double Half Hitches (#3 heading, page 24). Make small picots.

Turn work over. Do 2 rows Horizontal Double Half Hitches. Turn work over again. Do 1 row Horizontal Double Half Hitches*

#1 row, Double Square Knots
1 row, Square Knots alternating. At each edge of this row do 2 Reversed Double Half Hitches.
1 row, Double Square Knots
1 row, Horizontal Double Half Hitches
Turn work over. Do 1 row Horizontal Double Half Hitches.
Turn work over again. Do 1 row Horizontal Double Half Hitches #
Repeat # to # 4 times.
Repeat first 3 rows of Square Knots.
Repeat * to *. This completes the first side.

    Continue knotting for second side:
Do 27 rows Double Square Knots alternating, as shown in diagram.

To Finish: On reverse side, pull each two ends through the beginning loops, then thread the ends through the Horizontal Double Half Hitches.

Cut off excess ends. Sew one side. Reverse and insert pillow. Sew fourth side.

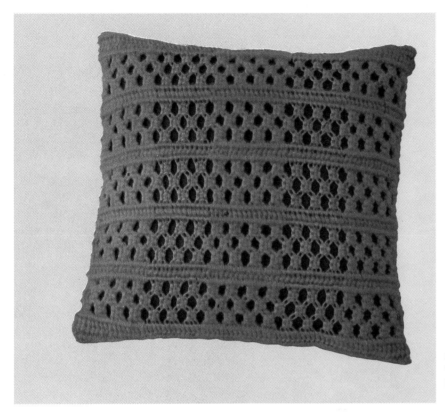

(Left) Front of red pillow cover worked in two different yarns. Note horizontal rows separating Square Knot areas.

(Right) Back of red pillow cover (also shown in detail on page 28). Note diagonal pattern created by Square Knots worked in alternate rows.

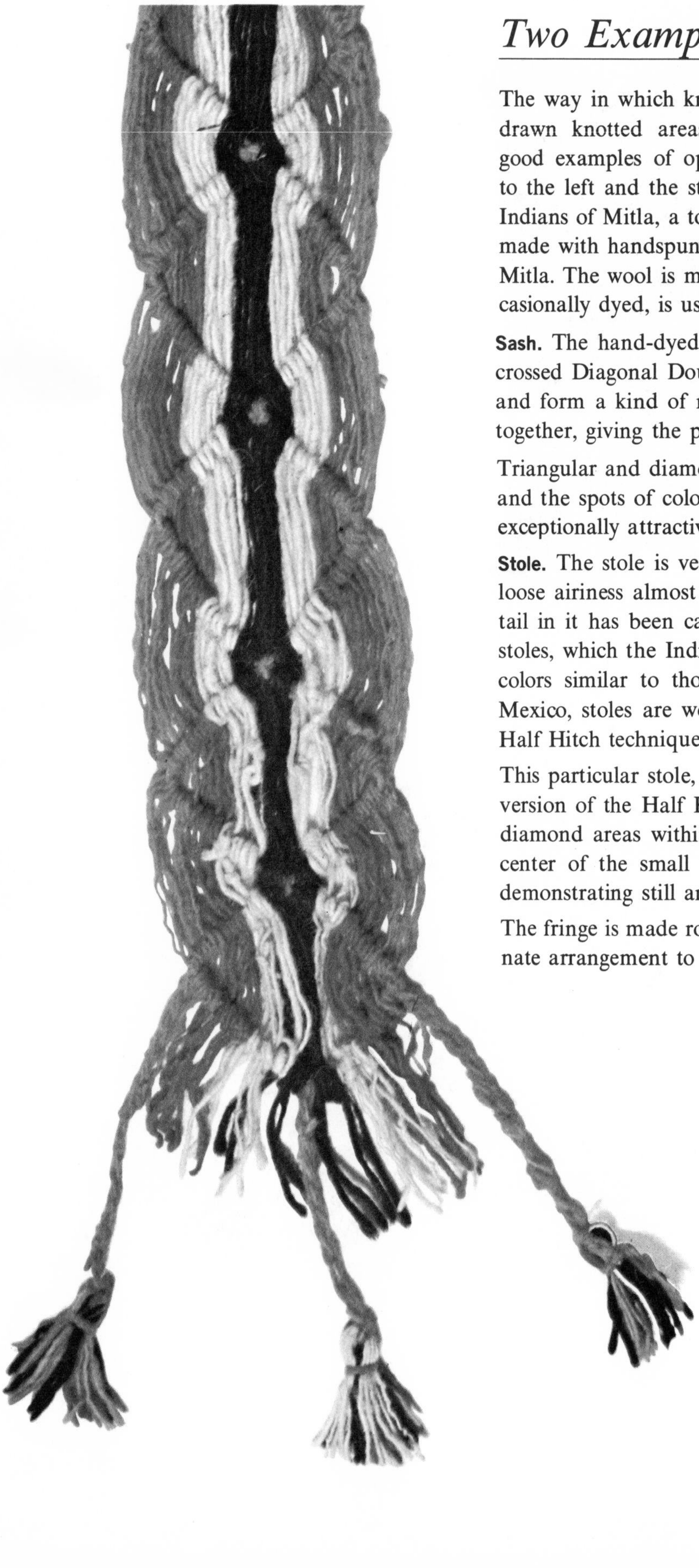

Two Examples From Mitla

The way in which knots are used determines the density of closely drawn knotted areas or the openness of unknotted areas. Two good examples of open-work are shown here in the colorful sash to the left and the stole on the facing page. They were knotted by Indians of Mitla, a town in the State of Oaxaca, Mexico. Both were made with handspun wools, as is much of the Macramé work from Mitla. The wool is mostly from sheep in the area and, although occasionally dyed, is usually left in its natural color.

Sash. The hand-dyed colors in the sash are bold and gay. Rows of crossed Diagonal Double Half Hitches are worked only at intervals and form a kind of network to hold the loose scallop-shaped ends together, giving the piece an orderly well-defined pattern.

Triangular and diamond-shaped designs make a strong appearance, and the spots of color at the crossings of the threads accentuate an exceptionally attractive design.

Stole. The stole is very luxurious-looking and has a lacy charm. Its loose airiness almost makes one unaware of the fact that every detail in it has been carefully developed. Very often these handsome stoles, which the Indians call *rebozos,* are done in a combination of colors similar to those used in the sash. Also, from this area of Mexico, stoles are worked, like the sash, completely in the Double Half Hitch technique.

This particular stole, however, is in natural wool and uses the Mitla version of the Half Knot to make the half-diamond bands and the diamond areas within which other diamonds are contained. In the center of the small diamonds, Overhand Knots are worked, thus demonstrating still another technique of creating an open area.

The fringe is made row by row, using an Overhand Knot in an alternate arrangement to tie each group of ends.

(Left) Detail of multicolor sash made by Indians of Mitla, Mexico. The wool is handspun, and is worked in crossed Diagonal Double Half Hitches.

(Facing page) Detail of stole in natural handspun wool—another example of open Macramé work from Mitla.

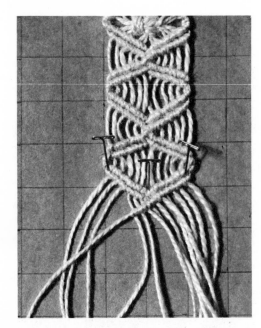

Sash is shown pinned to knotting board and against guidelines to keep proper width. Note method of crossing for Diagonal Double Half Hitches.

Sash #1 (Jute Sash)

To make a sash inspired by the work of the Mitla Indians, the Diagonal Double Half Hitch and the Square Knot with multiends are used. This combination is a useful and attractive way to achieve an open effect and an interesting pattern. The result is a handsome sash with weight and substance, and with somewhat the character of homespun work.

Size: 2″ x 80″, including fringes.

Materials: 1 cone Jute-Tone. #1 Chalk white. Lily Mills Co.

Knots: Horizontal and Diagonal Double Half Hitch, Square Knot using 10 ends, Double Chain Knot.

Cut Ends: 7 ends, each 9 yds. long.
No holding cord.

Directions: For the beginning fringe, make 8″ Double Chain Knot sinnets with every two ends—see example #9, pages 18–19.
With the middle two ends, take one end to the right. Make Horizontal Double Half Hitches across the row and back again to the middle. Repeat on left side.

Pattern: *Make a diamond with 2 rows of Diagonal Double Half Hitches*

#Make the top half of diamond. With center 10 ends make a Square Knot, using 2,6,2. Complete diamond # (A reminder: 2,6,2 means using 2 ends on either side and 6 ends as the core ends.)

Repeat * to *	Repeat # to # 3 times
Repeat # to # 3 times	Repeat * to * 3 times
Repeat * to * 3 times	Repeat # to # 3 times
Repeat # to # 5 times	Repeat * to * 3 times
Repeat * to * 3 times	Repeat # to # 5 times
Repeat # to # 3 times	Repeat * to *
Repeat * to * 3 times	

To Finish: Repeat the 2 rows of Horizontal Double Half Hitches, made as in the beginning, and the 8″ Double Chain Knot sinnets with every two ends.

(Below) Mitla-inspired sash made in jute—detail shown in actual size. Note that in some diamond areas the centers are gathered into a multiend Square Knot.

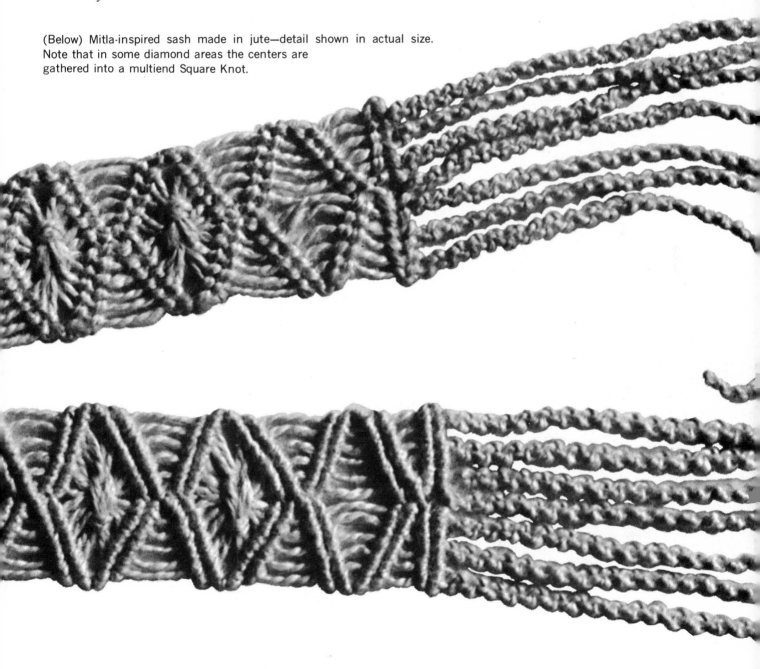

Sash #2 (Multicolor Sash)

This vivid three-colored sash, in a repeat diagonal design, is achieved primarily with the Diagonal Double Half Hitch Knot worked in a closely knotted pattern on both sides. An additional feature of this sash is the decorative use of the bobble.

This sash may be made as long as you wish by repeating the pattern.

Materials: 10/5 linen. Orange. Frederick J. Fawcett, Inc.
Avanti rug wool. Rose and black. Craft Yarns of Rhode Island, Inc.

Knots: Diagonal Double Half Hitch, Square Knot, Overhand Knot, and Bobble.

Width: Rose and orange— 4 ends each. Black—2 ends.

Arrange ends as follows, pinning each loop:
2 black, 4 rose, 8 orange, 4 rose, 2 black
Leave 14″ free before beginning to knot.

Multicolor sash with bobbles. The piece is worked on both sides with the Diagonal Double Half Hitch. The diagonal ridges are caused by working on the right side, the dotted pattern by working on the reverse side.

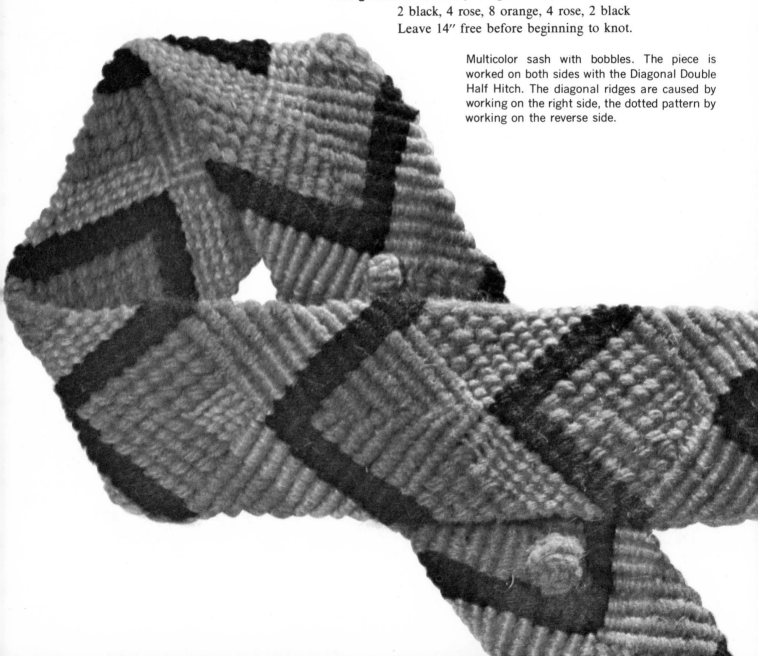

Directions: For beginning section.

With outside black end do Diagonal Double Half Hitches to center. Repeat with black end on other side.

Cross the two ends where they meet and continue in this manner for 3 rows, which brings four ends in rose to middle.

Make a bobble with the four center ends in rose, using 5 Square Knots (see diagram).

Continue with the Diagonal Double Half Hitch for 8 more rows. (This brings the four black ends to the middle.)

Make a bobble, using 5 Square Knots.

Turn piece over. Continue with Diagonal Double Half Hitches for 8 rows.

Turn piece over. Make an orange bobble.

Pattern Repeat: * Turn piece over. Do 10 rows Diagonal Double Half Hitches*.

Continue * to * until center section is of desired length. **Note:** Be sure to turn piece every 10 rows.

Directions: For ending section.

Make an orange bobble. Turn piece over and do 6 rows Diagonal Double Half Hitches.

Turn piece over and make a rose bobble

Turn piece over and do 4 rows Diagonal Double Half Hitches.

Turn piece to front and do 2 rows Diagonal Double Half Hitches.

Make a black bobble. Continue with Diagonal Double Half Hitches until there are 10 rows in all.

To Finish: Make Square Knot sinnets with remaining ends and tie them with a Gathering Knot.

MAKING A BOBBLE

Bobbles can be made to any size by changing the length of the Square Knot sinnet. They can also be made with multiend Square Knots. See diagram for construction.

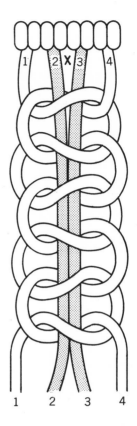

Bobble: With 3 or more Square Knots, make a sinnet. Bring core ends up to the beginning of the sinnet between ends #2 and #3 and draw through the space marked X. A crochet hook may be necessary. Pull core ends down firmly to complete bobble. Continue with whatever knot the pattern calls for.

Beginning of Belt #1. (Below) With four ends make #5 heading (page 24). Lay a new end over the Square Knot. Tie it in with a row of Horizontal Double Half Hitches, using all the ends. Take another end and continue in this fashion until there are twelve ends.

The last part of Belt #2.

Belt #1

Two belts are presented here. In the first you will be using another technique—the adding on of extra ends in order to widen a piece.

Finished Length: 34″. (For a longer or shorter belt, extend or reduce pattern areas.)

Materials: 10/5 linen. Natural. Frederick J. Fawcett, Inc.
2 loop buckles

Cut Ends: 6 ends, each 8 yds. long.

Knots: Square Knot and Horizontal Double Half Hitch.

To Begin: For construction of the beginning, see diagram at left.
Directions: * Do 6 rows Square Knots alternating.
Do 6 rows Double Square Knots alternating.
Make three sinnets of 6 Square Knots each.
Do 6 Reversed Square Knots on the two end threads on each side.
Make two sinnets of 6 Square Knots each, using the 8 remaining ends.
Make three sinnets of 6 Square Knots each *
Repeat * to *
Do 6 rows Square Knots alternating.
Do 6 rows Double Square Knots alternating.
Make three sinnets of 6 Square Knots each.

To Finish: Cut remaining ends, leaving about 6″. Put the ends over the loop buckles, with the back side of the belt facing you. Pull each four ends through each Square Knot. Tie each two ends with an Overhand Knot. Cut off remaining ends. When you put the beginning of the belt through the loop, the right side will show.

The last part of Belt #1.

Belt #2

You may make this belt to any length by following the directions.

Materials: 40/12 linen cable. Natural. William & Co. Brass buckles.

Knots and Key: Horizontal, Diagonal and Reversed Double Half Hitches—HDHH, DDHH, RDHH. Square Knot using multiends —SK. Diagonal Double Half Hitch crossing in middle—DDHHX.

Width: Cut 8 ends.

To Begin: Follow diagram.

Directions: 3 rows DDHHX, 5 rows DDHH
* 3 SK in the middle, tied 2,4,2. On either side do 5 rows DDHH knotted with four ends *
2 rows DDHHX
Repeat * to *
4 rows DDHHX
Repeat * to *, repeat # to #
§ Make two sinnets of 3 SK each tied 2,4,2. Add 1 SK made with center ends, 2,4,2 §
Repeat # to #, * to * as many times as necessary to complete back section for length desired, ending with # to #.
Repeat: § to §—# to #—* to *—# to #—* to *—# to #—* to *
1 row DDHHX, 3 rows DDHH, 4 rows DDHHX. 1 row HDHH as follows: cross ends in middle; take one end horizontally to the right and one end horizontally to the left.

To Finish: Put all ends over right buckle. Pull each end through to the back into the row of HDHH. Tie every four ends in a very tight Overhand Knot. Put Elmer's glue over knot. When it dries, cut ends.

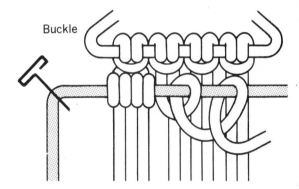

Buckle

The beginning of Belt #2. Put seven ends onto left buckle, using Reversed Double Half Hitches. With remaining end, do row of Horizontal Double Half Hitches as shown in the diagram. (Below) Starting point can be seen on finished belt on right side of buckle.

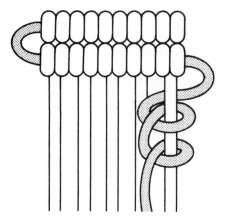

Vertical Double Half Hitches are used to change color from gold to blue.

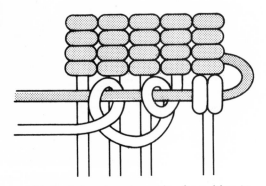

Method for changing color from blue to gold.

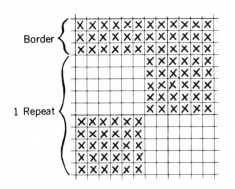

Key: X's = Horizontal Double Half Hitches. White squares = Vertical Double Half Hitches.

Rugs

The Double Half Hitch, when worked in a closely knotted pattern using heavy linen and/or wool as the yarns, produces sturdy and long-wearing mats and rugs. Because the knotting is kept simple, colors can play a large role in the design. Note, in the blue and gold rug section at right, how the Horizontal and Vertical Double Half Hitches create a checkerboard pattern and how vivid the ridged effects of these knots are. Both the front and back of the work are shown; either could be considered as the right side. The diagrams at left show how to change colors to achieve the pattern.

The use of this knot also makes it possible to chart a design on graph paper. Before making a graph, make samplers so that you will know the amount of ends to the inch.

The directions below are for a rug section of the size 9½″ x 15″. By adding to the length and width of the ends and by repeating the pattern, you can make any size desired. It is also possible to make a rug by working just in sections, and then joining them. Sections can be also made in squares.

blue and gold rug

Size: 9½″ x 15″ section

Materials: Pat rug wool. Blue #750, gold #17. Paternayan Bros., Inc.

Cut Ends: Gold—42, each 3 yds. 12″ long.

Holding Cord: Blue—203 yds. long, used also as knot-bearing cord. It will be necessary to splice this cord, since this amount of yarn will be too unwieldy for one butterfly. Cut the cord into sections and wind into butterflies.

Knots and Key: Horizontal and Vertical Double Half Hitches—HDHH, VDHH.

To Begin: Attach 3 rows HDHH to holding cord, using #2 heading (page 24).

Directions: * 6 HDHH, 6 VDHH. Repeat 3 times across row. End with 6 HDHH*

Repeat * to * 5 times.

6 VDHH, 6 HDHH. Repeat 3 times across row, ending with 6 VDHH

Repeat # to # 5 times.

Repeat * to * and # to # 5 times.

Repeat * to *

3 rows HDHH.

To Finish: Turn piece over. Thread in ends as shown in photograph.

Front

Method for threading in ends
with embroidery needle.

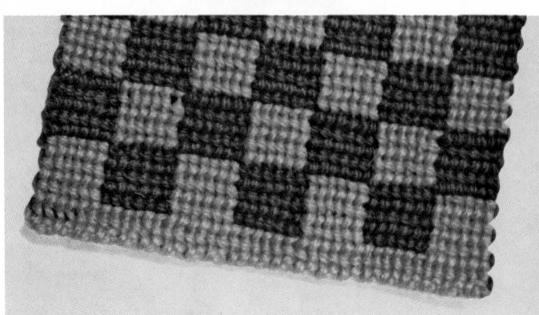

Back

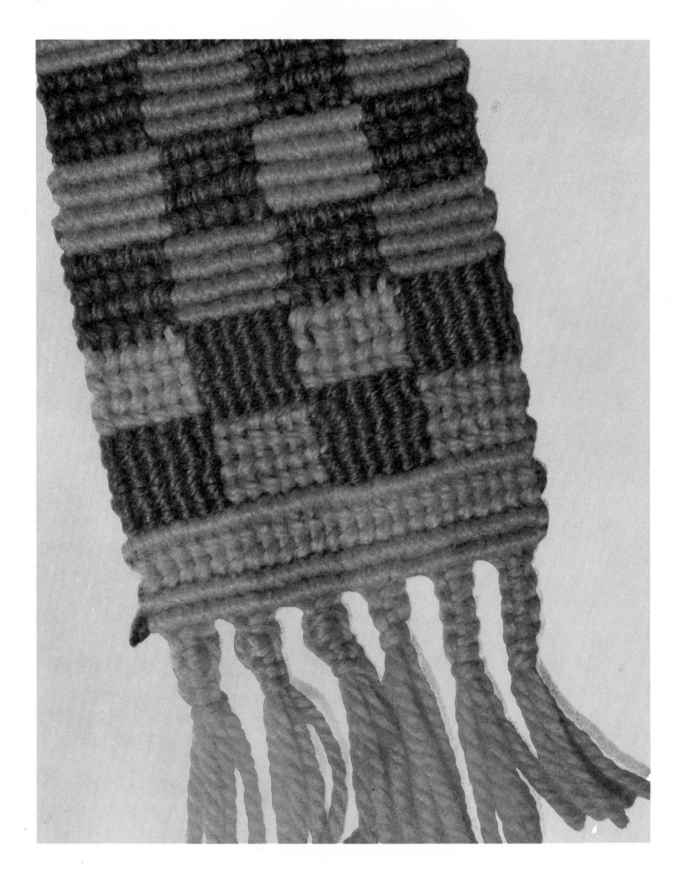

red rug

The red rug section in three colors shown here has the same checkerboard pattern as in the blue and gold rug section, but it is somewhat more advanced in technique. It also differs in the method of working, which affords a different surface texture. Again the variations and effects possible with the Double Half Hitch Knot are evident. The Horizontal and Vertical versions are used, and the variation is achieved by knotting from the front and then from the back. The end result makes the additional effort well worth while. The tying cords are of two colors, red and fuchsia; the third color, plum, is used as the knot-bearing cord. This rug section can be made by following the graph shown.

Size: 5″ x 14″ section, including fringe.

Material: Pat rug wool. Fuchsia #239, red #242, plum #610. Paternayan Bros., Inc.

Cut Ends: Fuchsia—6 ends, each 3 yds. 4″ long.
   Red—6 ends, each 3 yds. 4″ long.
   Plum—6 yds., for knot-bearing cord.
Each color area is knotted in the manner keyed by the graph.

KEY
HDHH = Horizontal Double Half Hitches
VDHH = Vertical Double Half Hitches
▬▬▬ HDHH knotted on front—1st color
- - - HDHH knotted on front—2nd color
● HDHH knotted on back—1st color
· HDHH knotted on back—2nd color
< VDHH knotted on front—3rd color
O HDHH knotted on back—3rd color

(Facing page) Red rug section. Each color area is knotted as indicated in the graph at upper right. Note that the pattern is worked on both front and back sides of the piece for added textural interest.

Helpful Hint.—To solve the problem of handling yarn in large bulk when making a larger rug section of heavy wool, you can knot from the center and work from two directions. First work in one direction. This means that the wound ends do not have to be as long and awkward to handle as they would be if the rug were worked from one side only. The photograph at right shows the method for beginning the section.

Cavandoli Stitch

The patterns on these two pages are examples of Macramé worked in the Cavandoli Stitch; information about the origin and background of this work is to be found in the Introduction. It consists of closely worked knotting in two colors. Just the Horizontal and Vertical Double Half Hitches are used—the former for background, the latter for design. This work is very unique and will enable you to chart and knot geometric shapes, trees, flowers, figures and so on to wherever your skill and imagination take you. Note the bird and plant figures on the Cavandoli-worked border for the Italian bag (see also page 6). A different-styled bird, influenced by a Mexican silver pin decoration, is presented in the graph below, right. The graph at left shows the possibility of obtaining a circular pattern effect. The curves are within the squares and are illusionary.

Border pattern for Italian bag in Cavandoli Stitch (bag is illustrated on page 6).

Bird Pattern

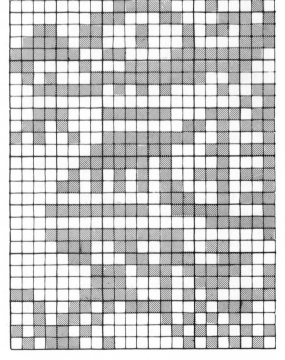

Circular Pattern

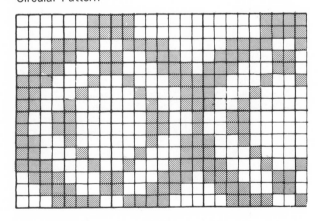

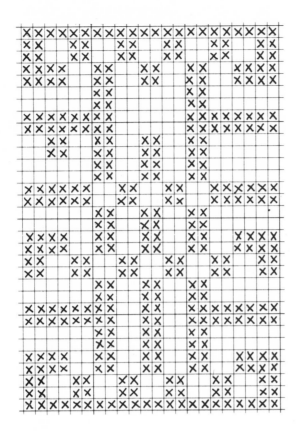

Geometric pattern. X's = Horizontal Double Half Hitches; white squares = Vertical Double Half Hitches.

black and white rug

The graph above is for the rug pattern and can be worked in different sizes. It is the simplest of the three graphs and is given with additional information. On all graphs, the dark areas represent the Horizontal Double Half Hitches and the light areas the Vertical Double Half Hitches. Note how identically the finished rug section pattern matches the graph.

Size: 4″ x 6″ section

Materials: 10/5 linen. Black. Frederick J. Fawcett, Inc.

Avanti rug wool. White. Craft Yarns of Rhode Island, Inc.

Cut Ends: Black—11 ends, each 48″ long.

Holding Cord, used also as knot-bearing cord: White, 4 yds. long.

To Begin: Attach ends to holding cord with #2 heading (page 24). In the 1st row the black cords are tied over the white cord. From then on go according to the graph so that sometimes you are tying black over white, and at other times white over black, depending on how the pattern is charted.

To Finish: Repeat the first row and make any fringe to your liking. The reverse side is equally handsome and, depending upon the effect you want, can be used for the right side.

Wall Hanging or Purse

The project presented here can be used in one of two ways: either as a wall hanging, or, with the sides attached, as a handsome purse. As in Sash #2 (page 48), the strong colors are used as contrasting bands that meet in the center and cross. The solid areas of the pattern are worked in the Diagonal Double Half Hitch (page 21, diagram D), and textural relief is supplied by the Square Knot.

Size: 7½″ x 20″

Materials: Avanti rug wool. Red, white, and black. Craft Yarns of Rhode Island, Inc.

    2 black dowels, 9¼″ long.

Cut Ends: Red—10 ends, each 6 yds. long.

    Black—10 ends, each 6 yds. long.

    White—8 ends, each 6 yds. long.

Knots: Square Knot and Diagonal Double Half Hitch.

To Begin: Arrange colors for knotting in this order: Red, white, black. Leave about 4″ of yarn before making sinnets of 6 Square Knots, using four ends each.

Directions to make top section:

Do 1 row Square Knots.

Drop two ends on each side and do 1 row Square Knots.

Continue making rows of Square Knots, dropping two ends on each row until the last Square Knot is made from the middle four ends. This will make a triangular area.

    To continue:

Pick up the dropped ends and make 20 rows of Diagonal Double Half Hitches with the ends crossing in the middle. (See pages 22–23 for angling technique.)

Turn piece over. Do 8 rows Diagonal Double Half Hitches crossing in the middle.

Turn piece over. Do 28 rows Diagonal Double Half Hitches. The knotted area now comes to a point. With the remaining ends on each side, fill in the areas with Square Knots until the piece is even across.

Make Square Knot sinnets as in the beginning.

Put sinnets over rods at both ends and thread ends in.

To Finish: Line with black cotton fabric, or color of your choice. For purse, sew sides 5½″ on each side.

Detail of finished purse.

Purse Handles:

Material: Black wool.

Cut Ends: 4 ends, each 48″ long.

Directions: With two ends make loops and attach with Reversed Double Half Hitch between 2nd and 3rd loops on dowel. The core ends should be 14″ long; the outside ends, 34″ long.

Make a sinnet of Square Knots, 12″ long. Loop sinnet over the rod, between last two loops; draw ends through to secure.

Repeat for second handle.

Same wall hanging becomes purse when sides are sewn together and handles are affixed.

(Left) Macramé piece used as wall hanging, with dowels at top and bottom.

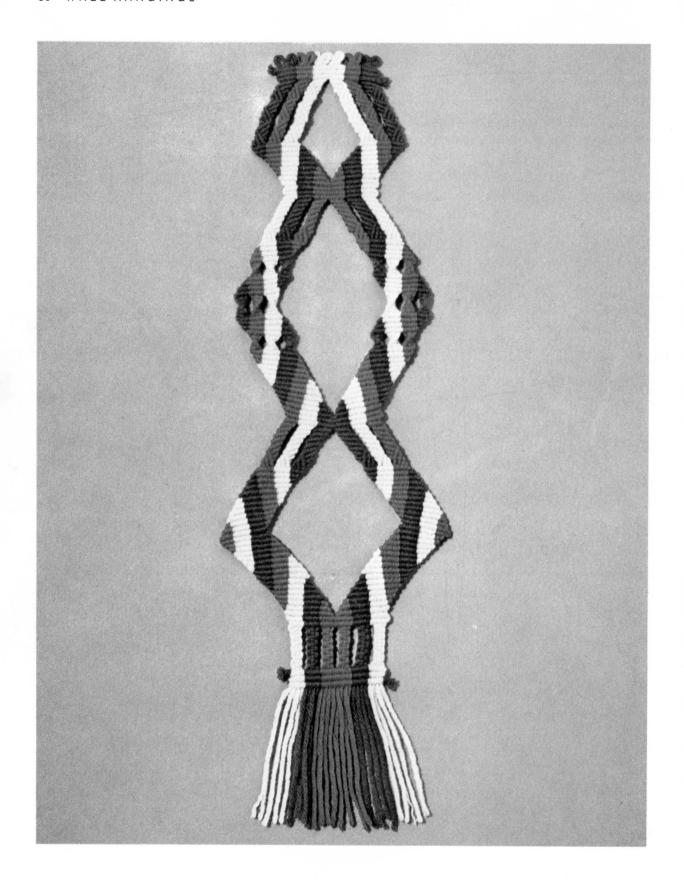

Wall Hangings Portfolio

A portfolio of hangings starts here and continues to page 77. It is hoped that these Macramé pieces will help you in creating your own designs. To help you further, "Christmas Bells", pages 70–71, is given with full directions. All others are analyzed so that you may see how knots are combined and progress in their many variations. Note that the hangings are bisymmetrical: whatever is worked on one side is also worked on the other.

spirit of '76

6¼'' x 27''

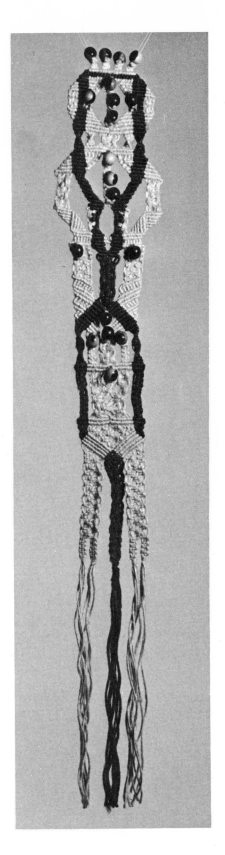

The wall hanging in red, white, and blue rug wool on the facing page could be considered an exercise in angling and color (see pages 22–23). The knots used were the Square Knot and the Horizontal Double Half Hitch. The piece was started on a wooden bar and its knotting was duplicated for the ending. The colors are all strong in value so that they provide good contrast where they cross. The pattern was kept simple to avoid any conflict with the colors.

All the colors are easy to follow, but, taking the white as an example, note how it starts in the middle, separates towards the right and left, and disappears only to reappear and repeat the pattern.

By the continuation of Horizontal Double Half Hitch rows, the white was worked at the end to the right and left. Sinnets were made of each color, and a holding cord was added, onto which three rows of Horizontal Double Half Hitches were made. The ends were trimmed, giving a plain fringe consistent with the simplicity of the piece.

amigo

5½'' x 33''

The color of handmade wooden beads from Morelia, Mexico, contributed handsomely towards the design of Amigo (right) and harmonized with the brown and natural 1½ lea linen. The beads were used in the heading along with Double Square Knots. Brown linen was introduced during rows of Horizontal and Vertical Double Half Hitches. The beads in the middle were added between Triple Square Knots. Construction continued, using the above knots and more beads.

The ending could be a simple piece by itself. Two rows of Horizontal Double Half Hitches precede a triangle of Square Knots. These are enclosed by Diagonal Double Half Hitches. The sinnets at the finish are ended with Square Knots and are pulled together with a Gathering Knot.

bill's folly

6″ x 10″
Collection of the Penland School of Crafts

This hanging (left), in three colors, is a good exercise for beginners. Square Knots with multiends and Horizontal Double Half Hitches were used. It could be very welcome as a thank-you present or as a baby christening gift.

The yarns are natural 1½ lea linen and rug wool. A flat bar of hardwood was used in place of a holding cord to mount the starting ends. The sides were knotted in Horizontal Double Half Hitches. The center repeated the Horizontal Double Half Hitch pattern, and a bobble (see page 49) was knotted in for additional interest. To the right and left of the center, multiend Square Knots were made, followed by rows of Square Knots and an area of Horizontal Double Half Hitches angled.

For the finish the piece was pulled together by two rows of Horizontal Double Half Hitches. Sinnets were made with Square Knots, ending with an Overhand Knot.

animal fair

Approx. 2″ x 18″

The three wall hangings on the facing page were made with children in mind and were presented to my nephew and two nieces for Christmas. The oldest child was then six years old.

The materials used were plied linen and lightweight rug wool. Each piece is different, but they all have the following knots in common: Square Knots, Overhand Knots, Reversed, Vertical, Diagonal and Horizontal Double Half Hitches, and bobbles.

The pieces were started on wooden napkin rings hand-carved into animal shapes by craftsmen in North Carolina. I purchased these at the Craftsmen of the Southern Highlands Guild Shop in Asheville. Searching out and using handcrafted items, such as these, brings excitement and pleasure to the knotter as well as contributing a new dimension to the work. Wall hangings such as these make excellent boutique items.

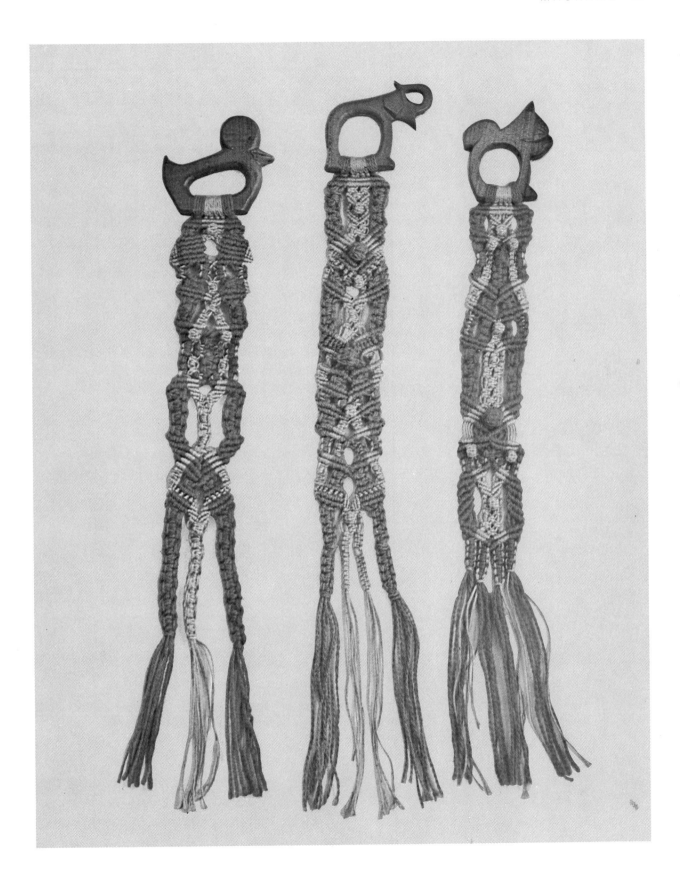

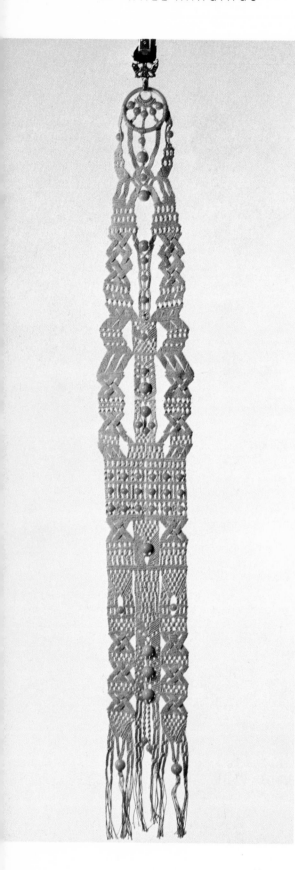

peking

8″ x 55″
Collection of Mrs. Glenn A. Stackhouse

Another approach to consider is combining interesting old jewelry with yarns as illustrated by the wall hanging on these pages. Old Peking glass beads of two sizes, a bracelet, and a ring were used. This piece is among my favorites because it was an adventure just to find the beads hidden under a counter and in the basement of one of the old shops in San Francisco's Chinatown. The bracelet and ring were found in still another fascinating shop. With these adornments as starting points, I used a matching color in 10/5 yellow linen to further enhance the beads for the design I had planned.

The piece was started on the small ring using Reversed Double Half Hitches. Two rows of Horizontal Double Half Hitches followed, then a row of Square Knots. Five small beads were added. Additional knotting was done before the bracelet was added. All the ends were then attached by a row of Horizontal Double Half Hitches, and the top part of the wall hanging was completed.

The work progressed by keeping the sides and center as separate points of interest. On the right and left sides, beads were put on, then flanked by Reversed Double Half Hitches going into rows of Horizontal Double Half Hitches; these were followed by Square Knots and Overhand Knots, all ending in a section of Horizontal Double Half Hitches. The center section used beads in two different sizes and narrow bands of Horizontal Double Half Hitches.

The piece was then brought together by a couple of rows of Horizontal Double Half Hitches and a small bead, followed by narrow bands worked in variations on the Horizontal Double Half Hitch. Square Knots and Overhand Knots were then worked, divided by rows of Horizontal Double Half Hitches.

Three sections again became separate units. In the center, narrow bands of Horizontal Double Half Hitches were made, and beads, divided by Square Knots, were added. On the outside areas, alternating and crossing bands of Double Half Hitches were angled. This section was ended with Square Knots, Overhand Knots, then small units of Horizontal Double Half Hitches, followed by several rows done in the same knot.

Again the piece divided into three sections. Double Half Hitches, angling and crossing, are on the outside, and in the center are Square Knots, Overhand Knots, Horizontal and Reversed Double Half Hitches, and beads of two sizes.

(Left) Detail of heading section of Peking, showing how ends were mounted onto a small ring. Note the color blend of both the yarn and the jewelry pieces.

(Below) Detail of center section. Note alternating and crossing bands of angled Double Half Hitches on outside areas. Horizontal Double Half Hitches join this section at beginning and end.

The section that follows could be considered for a separate wall hanging. Rows of Horizontal Double Half Hitches, Square Knots, Overhand Knots, and twisted Half Knots form borders for rows of small beads.

The last section is in three parts. The outside areas begin by crossing and progress to Square Knots and Overhand Knots in alternating sections. The center has a diamond area of Double Square Knots. These go into solid areas of Horizontal Double Half Hitches with a bead in the middle. The entire section is held together with several rows of Horizontal Double Half Hitches.

Traveling downward, the side and center sections were formed into open areas by Double Square Knots, and Square Knots with Overhand Knots. Rows of Horizontal Double Half Hitches also were worked. The side sections progressed to crossed areas divided by Double Square Knots and Horizontal Double Half Hitches. The center progressed from Square Knots and Overhand Knots to Horizontal Double Half Hitches interspersed with beads. The ends are sinnets of Square Knots and twisting Half Knots and embrace the same principle as the ending of Amigo on page 61.

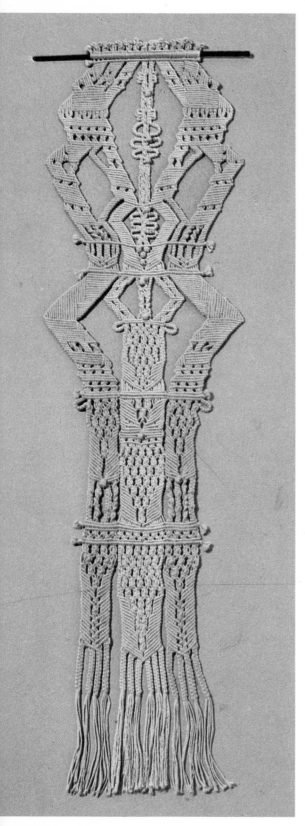

empress

9½″ x 33″

Picots, prominently placed in the top half of the center area, contribute a looped ribbon effect to this regal-appearing wall hanging. Still another specific decorative approach is added by bobbles and more picots appearing occasionally on the edges. The yarns used are yellow linen and natural silk cord. The piece was started with the #5 heading (see page 24), a crownlike effect which served to introduce and to accentuate the picot theme. After being knotted, the heading was mounted onto an old teak chopstick.

The center section, in the natural silk twist, besides being worked in a variety of picots and bobbles, also contains Square Knots, Overhand Knots, and Reversed Double Half Hitches. In addition, there are angled areas of Double Half Hitches. The side areas in yellow linen are dominated by angling Double Half Hitches, Square Knots, Half Knots, Overhand Knots, and sinnets of Half Knots that twist in opposite directions.

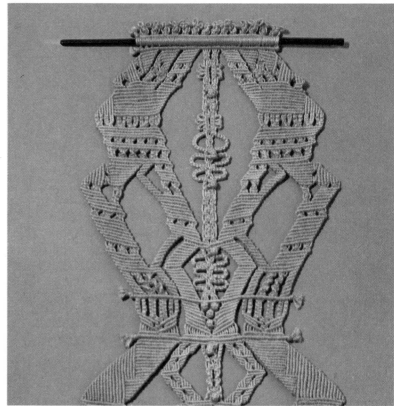

(Above) Enlarged detail of top section, showing the decorative use of picots and bobbles.

In the bottom half of the hanging, the yellow and white areas appear separate, but while the colors are independent of each other, the design is not. The beginning of this area is a good example of the variations that can be obtained by angling the Double Half Hitch Knot. As stated previously, the Half Hitch is the most practical knot for obtaining variations.

The knots used here are the same as those worked in the top half of the piece, but the effect is a contrasting one due to the arrangement of the design. The top was worked as if the sections were independent of one another, although the knots formed a continuous and similar pattern, whereas the knots in the bottom half were worked straight across the rows to form a unit. The piece ends in Square Knot sinnets.

summer sun

6" x 35"

Collection of the Penland School of Crafts

One of the unique features of this wall hanging is the development of its shape from a narrow heading at the top to an increased width as the piece is worked. The addition of extra ends throughout the growth of the top half accounts for its gradual widening. This technique, which was used in Belt #1 (page 50–51), is a very practical one in Macramé work for developing small rounded or pointed areas.

The yarns used are rug wool and 1½ lea linen, both in different shades of yellow. The piece was started on a Peking glass ring which immediately limited the number of starting ends that could be used effectively. In the top half, the edges were developed in wool, and the remaining area in linen. In the linen area, additional ends were put on to begin increasing the width of the piece. Additional ends were also put on in the wool areas and were used in Vertical Double Half Hitches next to rows of Horizontal Double Half Hitches. Bobbles were interspersed for added textural interest.

Separate sinnets were made of linen and of wool and of a combination of the two materials. The crossed area was done in a combination of Horizontal Double Half Hitches and sinnets, and multiend Square Knots. The rest of the piece was made up of variations on the Horizontal Double Half Hitch and Square Knot. The piece was finished with sinnets, each made up of a variation on the knots used.

stately mansion

7½'' x 42''

Two distinguishable design elements are very evident here, and they are further accentuated by the rows of Horizontal Double Half Hitches that serve to separate them. The angling technique of the Double Half Hitch Knot (see pages 22–23) makes the planning of distinctive pieces possible and by its use clearly illustrates how Macramé work can be developed to express an idea, much like a painting. This wall hanging is presented as an excellent example of the use of this knot in one of its many variations.

The yarns were two kinds of silk used double, wool singly, and 1½ lea linen double. The knots were the Double Half Hitch in its many variations, and the Square Knot for making bobbles.

The first patterned design appears in the top section of the piece and consists firstly of three areas of Square Knot bobbles in wool. These are interspersed with other areas made up of crisscrossed bands done by varying the Horizontal Double Half Hitch Knot. The combination of these two different knotted areas results in a strong diamond effect which looks as though it had been interwoven. This section can be seen in detail in the upper photograph on the facing page. Following the area described, more crisscrossed bands were worked and were held together with rows of Horizontal Double Half Hitches.

The second design area was worked in a manner completely different from any of the other hangings that have been shown. Note that the lower detail photograph on the facing page clearly shows the twisted areas of this unique pattern. By working variations on the Horizontal Double Half Hitch throughout this entire piece, it was possible to knot what appears as three different columns, all made with separate twists. For the center column, two strips were knotted separately, then twisted, and then knotted again with the Horizontal Double Half Hitch traveling in different directions, until they were knotted together to form one column.

The two columns on the sides were each composed of two different-sized strips. Each pair of strips was knotted separately until they reached a midpoint where they were joined. They continued to grow with Diagonal Double Half Hitches until they, and the center column, met at the beginning of the next section.

More areas of crisscrossed bands were accomplished by working the Horizontal Double Half Hitch Knot in a partial repeat of the first design. This was followed by a repeat with variations on the second design. Either of these two designs could be chosen to make an effective smaller hanging, or they could be a starting point for your own ideas.

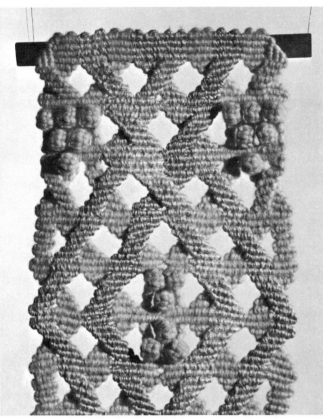

(Left) Detail of top section of Stately Mansion clearly shows the angling technique of the Double Half Hitch Knot (explained on pages 22–23). Bobbles are clustered for added decorative effect.

(Right) Detail of center section, showing how six bands were joined together at midpoint to make three columns. Note twist of center column.

christmas bells

This gay holiday wall hanging is presented with full directions. The important feature here is in the play of color between the red and green bands, and the contrast between the solid areas of knotting and the open spaces. Both the knotting pattern and the design were kept simple so as not to conflict with the colors.

Size: 4¼″ x 49″

Materials: #1 Rattail rayon. Red, grey, moss green. Fibre Yarn Co. 19 brass bells

Cut Ends: 4 ends of each color, each 22 yds. long.
Holding Cord, also used as knot-bearing cord: 1 end of grey, 18″ long.

Knots and Key: Square Knot—SK, and Horizontal, Diagonal, Vertical and Reversed Double Half HItches—HDHH, DDHH, VDHH, RDHH. Diagonal Double Half Hitch Crossing—DDHHX.

Top section. Note triangular area of Square Knots and how dropped ends were worked into diagonal rows of Double Half Hitches.

Detail shows color changes from one side to the other and open areas.

To Begin: Make Square Knots on a holding cord (#4 heading, page 24), using 8 red, 8 grey and 8 green.

Do 2 rows HDHH.

Do 1 row across of HDHH in red, VDHH in grey, and HDHH in green.

Do 1 row HDHH.

The beginning of the piece is now completed.

Directions: Do 1 row SK, drop two ends on each side, and do another row SK. Continue in this manner, dropping two ends on each side until 1 SK is left.

Put a bell on the core ends of the last knot.

This completes the triangle of Square Knots.

Pick up the dropped ends and do 4 rows DDHHX.

Do 1 row SK.

Do 4 rows DDHHX.

* In the center, put two bells onto core ends of green and red. Do 1 row SK, 2 rows DDHHX; put bell on the two ends that cross. Do 2 rows DDHHX. Do 1 row SK *

Fringe to finish off piece, using variation on Square Knots.

8 rows DDHHX, repeat * to *	4 rows DDHH
8 rows DDHH	1 row SK
1 row SK	4 rows DDHH, repeat * to *
4 rows DDHH, repeat * to *	6 rows DDHHX
8 rows DDHHX	1 row SK
1 row SK	4 rows DDHHX
4 rows DDHH	1 row SK
1 row SK	4 rows DDHHX
8 rows DDHH, repeat * to *	1 row SK
8 rows DDHHX	8 rows DDHHX, repeat * to *
1 row SK	4 rows DDHHX
4 rows DDHH	1 row SK
1 row SK	8 rows DDHHX

To Finish: Make the fringe by first traveling from the left to the middle in the following manner:

3 SK—red	2 SK—(2 red and 2 grey ends)
1 SK—grey	2 SK—(2 grey and 2 green ends)
1 SK—green	4 SK—each of red, grey, and green
2 SK—(2 red and 2 grey ends)	2 RDHH—red
2 RDHH—red	2 SK—(2 red and 2 grey ends)
2 SK—(2 red and 2 grey ends)	2 SK—(2 grey and 2 green ends)
2 SK—(2 grey and 2 green ends)	9 SK—red
4 SK—each of red, grey, and green	12 SK—grey
2 RDHH—red	14 SK—green

Finish sinnets with a Gathering Knot and trim ends.

Repeat directions for opposite side, working from right to middle.

cascade

8½″ x 47″

The combination of two yarns of completely different weights and qualities, and the excitement generated by the interplay between such a combination, provide the outstanding characteristics of this wall hanging. An effect which is a sharp departure from what one usually expects to find in Macramé work is also created by the use of these yarns; for even though the knotting pattern is very obvious, one is more conscious of the yarns used. Therefore, this hanging serves to illustrate the effect that yarns can have in a finished piece.

The yarns used were 12/16 linen cable and heavy wool roving. To begin the piece, the wool roving was mounted onto a hardwood bar with the Reversed Double Half Hitch. A row of Vertical Double Half Hitches served to introduce the linen cable, which was used double throughout. One row of Square Knots was then made with the roving, and additional linen was put on with a row of Vertical Double Half Hitches. Another row of Square Knots was done, and new ends of linen, using the Reversed Double Half Hitch, were added between the second and third Square Knots.

More linen was added on a row of Horizontal Double Half Hitches, using the Reversed Double Half Hitch. From here on bobbles were made and the wool and linen areas appear to be independent of each other.

Square Knots were worked with the linen, using the roving as the core ends. Additional sections of linen were knotted, and then sections of roving, ending with the linen worked over the roving.

KNOTTING PATTERN

In the detail photograph, the section of the wall hanging which follows is shown with certain areas designated as **A, B,** and **C** in order that you may see more clearly how the knots progressed.

Section **A** shows the definite interplay that was worked between the two areas of linen and roving. Also in this section, the Square Knots can be seen tied in two different directions, the second being the reverse of the first.

Section **B** illustrates an example of Square Knots being made with the linen over the roving to give a wrapping effect.

Section **C** shows Square Knot areas of linen worked independently of the wool. The wool areas are knotted behind the linen. The linen and wool are worked together again as the piece progresses.

The ending of the piece was made with a row of Horizontal Double Half Hitches, a row of Vertical Double Half Hitches in roving, a row of Vertical Double Half Hitches in linen, then a row of Square Knots in roving, followed by a row of Vertical Double Half Hitches in linen.

For a fringe effect, the roving was made into sinnets of Square Knots. The linen was used to tie the Square Knots with the roving as the core ends.

Enlarged detail of center section.

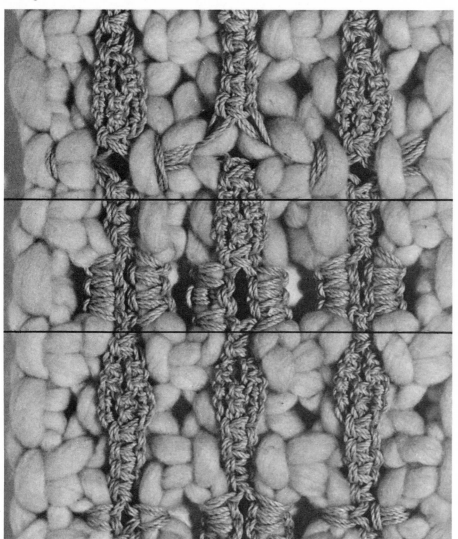

A

B

C

nightbird

5½" x 36"
Collection of Paul Hodges Allen, Jr.

The versatility of the Horizontal Double Half Hitch Knot is here again demonstrated by still another distinctive pattern obtained by using one of its variations. The most important and interesting section of this wall hanging is another departure from the knotted patterns of the other hangings that have been presented thus far. A scallop-shaped design was accomplished by using the Double Half Hitch in angling and alternating patterns. Still another design feature of this piece is the way in which the wooden beads were used to accentuate triangular patterns. Since the design was such an intricate one, only one color was used, causing the beads that are of a brighter value to stand out distinctly.

The materials used were 1½ lea linen and wooden beads. This yarn is not recommended for the beginning knotter since it frays easily, but, when handled with care, it gives a wonderful look to the finished piece that would not be obtainable with a plied yarn.

A #6 heading (see page 24) was made and then mounted onto a holding cord with a row of Horizontal Double Half Hitches. The ends were then attached to a dowel, using the Horizontal Double Half Hitch. Next another row of Horizontal Double Half Hitches was mounted onto a holding cord, followed by two rows of Square Knots alternating. At either edge, picots were made during the tying in of rows of Reversed Double Half Hitches. The area in the center was formed into a triangular shape by the use of Square Knots alternating. This shape was emphasized by putting in a border of wooden beads.

To complete this first section, triple and quadruple Square Knot sinnets were made. They were all tied together by rows of Diagonal Double Half Hitches which were then underlined with a row of beads. Then another, larger, triangular-shaped area was made, again using the Square Knot.

The unique pattern of this piece was now worked. In this, Double Half Hitches angled were tied in and were alternated, so that some were horizontal and others were vertical, often both in the same row. This resulted in the scallop-shaped design mentioned above.

The next area consists of Double Square Knots alternating. The beads were incorporated into the knotting to form a triangle. The result is in part illusionary since the beads are used in just the top and bottom areas.

The ending began with two rows of Horizontal Double Half Hitches. A row of Double Square Knots was made and then a straight row of beads was put on. A row of Double Square Knots followed, with three rows of Horizontal Double Half Hitches. Sinnets were made of three Double Square Knots each. The ends were allowed to hang long and free and were interspersed at intervals with beads and then trimmed off neatly to finish.

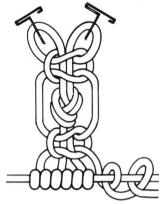

Top section of wall hanging. A row of #6 heading (page 24) was mounted onto a holding cord. Ends were then knotted onto a dowel.

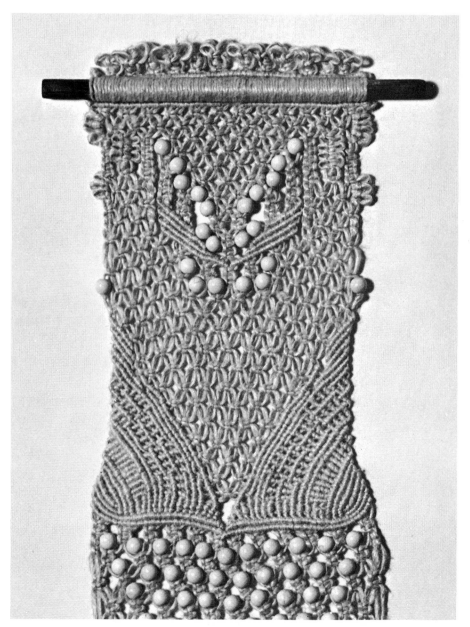

gazebo

38″ long x 24″ around

The hanging here is not a wall hanging but a circular three-dimensional suspended form. It was chosen to end the section on wall hangings in order to demonstrate once again the enormous scope of this craft. There is a sculptural quality to this piece which is due in part to its shape and in part to the use of basically simple knots in elaborate patterns. Also, since it is free-hanging, the added quality of motion adds a new interest.

The yarns used were 12/16 linen cable and 5/1 linen, the latter using multiends as one end. Two light, neutral colors were used because of the intricate knotting patterns and small white wooden beads were chosen to harmonize with the design.

The starting ends were bound together at the top, and the knotting was begun from that point (this is a departure from conventional methods). A holding cord and a length of fine wire were coupled together and the beads were knotted on. The rigidity of the wire and the beads combined to form the beginning of the circular shape. As the knotting progressed, additional ends of linen were put on so

that the piece could continue to grow in width. Beads and wire were added throughout this top area to help with the development of the shape.

A number of different knots were used in this section. Bobbles were added at the top and ended in Square Knot areas. These were secured by two rows of Horizontal Double Half Hitches. More areas of knots followed, using Double Half Hitch and Square Knots alternating. Beads continued to be added onto the rows of Horizontal Double Half Hitches, which in turn were separated by Square Knots. A group of Square Knots using multiends were put on, followed by an area of Half Knot sinnets worked with right and left twists. This entire section can be seen in the detail photograph at lower left on the facing page.

This area was then pulled together with two rows of Horizontal Double Half Hitches, completing the domelike top of the piece. For the next two areas the piece was designed to narrow; therefore beads and wire were not added.

Within these areas the knotting pattern began with Reversed Double Half Hitches and Square Knots, followed by two rows of Horizontal Double Half Hitches, which ended the first section. The second area was worked in alternate rows of Square Knots using eight ends. These sections are shown in the detail photograph at lower right on the facing page.

With the completion of the narrowed section, more beads and wire were added onto rows of Horizontal Double Half Hitches, to maintain the circular shaping and to enable the piece to grow in width. This wider area was patterned after the top domelike section.

The ending of the piece was done by making Square Knot sinnets, multiend Square Knots, and additional Square Knot sinnets. The ends were then left to hang free with beads added at intervals.

(Facing page, left) Detail of domelike top section. Note Square Knot sinnets and Half Knot twisting left-right, right-left. Note also arrangement of wooden beads.

(Facing page, right) Detail of center narrowed section. Note alternating Square Knot sinnets and alternate rows of Square Knots using eight ends. These areas are separated by two rows of Horizontal Double Half Hitches.

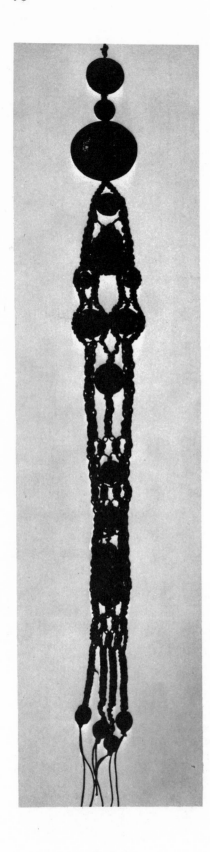

Index

bobble	49
butterfly	15
core ends	16–17
Diagonal Double Half Hitch	21
Double Chain Knot	18–19
Double Half Hitch	20–21
Double Half Hitch—angling technique	22–23
Double Square Knot	32–33
end (individual length of yarn)	14
Gathering Knot	25
Half Hitch	18–19
Half Knot	16–17
hand bobbin	15
headings	24–25
holding cord (horizontal length of yarn to mount ends on)	15
Horizontal Double Half Hitch	20
knot-bearing cord (cord that ends are tied over)	14
knotting board	10
Overhand Knot	18–19
Picots	24–25
Reversed Double Half Hitch	18–19
sinnets	16–17, 18–19
splicing (adding yarn to ends)	25
Square Knot	16–17
Square Knot reversed	16–17
Square Knot—alternating technique	32–33
Square Knot with multiends	25
Vertical Double Half Hitch	21

Bibliography

BOOKS

Anchor Manual of Needlework, 2nd ed., B. T. Batsford, Ltd., London, England, 1966.

Ashley, Clifford, W., *The Ashley Book of Knots,* Doubleday & Co., Garden City, N.Y., 1944.

De Dillmont, Thérèse, *Encyclopedia of Needlework,* Mulhouse, Alsace, France (no date).

De Dillmont, Thérèse, *Le Macramé,* Mulhouse, Alsace, France (no date).

Graumont, Raoul, and Wenstrom, Elmer, *Square Knot Handicraft Guide,* Cornell Maritime Press. Cambridge, Maryland, 1949.

Graumont, Raoul, and Hensel, John, *Encyclopedia of Knots and Fancy Rope Work,* 4th ed., Cornell Maritime Press, Cambridge, Maryland, 1952.

Groves, Sylvia, *The History of Needlework Tools and Accessories,* Country Life, Ltd., London, 1966.

Harvey, Virginia I., *Macramé, The Art of Creative Knotting,* Van Nostrand Reinhold Co., New York, N.Y., 1967.

May, Florence Lewis, *Hispanic Lace & Lace Making,* Hispanic Society of America, New York, N.Y., 1939.

Sylvia's Book of Macramé Lace (ca. 1882–1885).

PERIODICALS

Craft Horizons (published by the American Craftsmen's Council), 16 East 52nd Street, New York, N.Y. 10022.

Handweaver & Craftsman, 220 Fifth Avenue, New York, N.Y. 10001.

Film Services

Research Dept., American Crafts Council 29 West 53rd Street, New York, N.Y. 10019

Book Services

Craft and Hobby Book Service P.O. Box 626, Pacific Grove, Calif. 93950

The Yarn Depot 545 Sutter Street, San Francisco, Calif. 94102

The Unicorn, Books for Craftsmen P.O. Box 645, Rockville, Md. 20851

P. C. Herwig Company 264 Clinton Street, Brooklyn, N.Y. 11201

Museum Books, Inc. 48 East 43rd Street, New York, N.Y. 10017

K. R. Drummond 30 Hart Grove, Ealing Common, London, W.5, Eng.

Suppliers

For linen yarns:
Frederick J. Fawcett, Inc.
129 South Street
Boston, Massachusetts 02111

For wool yarns:
Paternayan Bros., Inc.
312 East 95th Street
New York, N.Y. 10028

William Condon & Sons, Ltd.
65 Queen Street
Charlottetown, P.O. Box 129
Prince Edward Island, Canada

For assorted yarns:
The Yarn Depot (also "T" pins)
545 Sutter Street
San Francisco, California 94102

Craft Yarns of Rhode Island, Inc.
603 Mineral Spring Avenue
Pawtucket, Rhode Island 02862

Lily Mills Co.
Dept. HWH
Shelby, North Carolina 28150

Fibre Yarn Co., Inc.
840 Sixth Avenue
New York, N.Y. 10001

The Niddy Noddy
1 Croton Point Avenue
Croton-on-Hudson, New York 10520

I. B. Silk Co.
315 West 36th Street
New York, N.Y. 10018

For buckles, rings and "T" pins:
Walco Toy Co., Inc.,
38 West 37th St.,
New York, N.Y. 10018

Greenberg & Hammer, Inc.
24 West 57th Street
New York, New York 10022

P. C. Herwig Co.
264 Clinton Street
Brooklyn, New York 11201

Schools and Workshops

The following is a partial list of schools and workshops that offer courses in Macramé from time to time. For further information write to the school direct.

Pendleton Fabric Craft School
Box 233
Sedona, ARIZONA 86336

Everywoman's Village
5634 Sepulveda Boulevard
Van Nuys, CALIFORNIA 91401

Mendocino Art Center
P.O. Box 36
Mendocino, CALIFORNIA 95460

San Jose State College
125 South 7th Street
San Jose, CALIFORNIA 95114

The Yarn Depot, Inc.
545 Sutter Street
San Francisco, CALIFORNIA 94102

Brookfield Crafts Center
Brookfield, CONNECTICUT 06804

Willimantic Summer Arts & Crafts Workshop
(Eastern State Conn. College)
Willimantic, CONNECTICUT 06220

Indiana University
Fine Arts Building
Bloomington, INDIANA 47401

School of the Wichita Art Association
9112 East Central
Wichita, KANSAS 67206

Haystack Mountain School of Crafts
Deer Island, MAINE 07043

Bloomfield Art Association
1516 Cranbrook Road
Birmingham, MICHIGAN 48009

Garrison Art Center
Garrison, NEW YORK 10524

Crafts Students League
West Side YWCA
840 Eighth Avenue
New York, NEW YORK 10019

The Niddy Noddy
1 Croton Point Avenue
Croton-on-Hudson, NEW YORK 10520

Penland School of Crafts
Penland, NORTH CAROLINA 28765

Arts & Crafts Society
616 N.W. 19th Avenue
Portland, OREGON 97209

Contemporary Crafts Gallery
3934 S.W. Corbett Avenue
Portland, OREGON 97201

The Mannings
Creative Crafts School
R.R.2
East Berlin, PENNSYLVANIA 17316

Arrowmont School of Arts & Crafts
Box 567
Gatlinburg, TENNESSEE 37738